Landlords Are People Too

Landlords Are People Too

A Tongue-in-Cheek Memoir of a Landlord in the Big Apple

Carl Rosenberg

iUniverse, Inc.
Bloomington

Landlords Are People Too
A Tongue-in-Cheek Memoir of a Landlord in the Big Apple

iUniverse books may be ordered through booksellers or by contacting:

iUniverse
1663 Liberty Drive
Bloomington, IN 47403
www.iuniverse.com
1-800-Authors (1-800-288-4677)

ISBN: 978-1-4620-6388-8 (sc)
ISBN: 978-1-4620-6390-1 (hc)
ISBN: 978-1-4620-6389-5 (ebk)

Printed in the United States of America

iUniverse rev. date: 01/12/2012

CONTENTS

Acknowledgements:

I WANT TO GIVE special thanks to my wife Rivka, my daughter Lisa, and my son Benjamin. Without their support this book would never have been written. Also, I can't forget to include my friend Dennis, who wouldn't let me give up when I felt my task was too overwhelming to continue.

Introduction

THERE ARE TWO REASONS I wrote this book. The first reason was to release the tension that has been steadily building up within me over the years. The second reason was to dispel the preconceived notion of many that landlords are greedy, money-grubbing, heartless, and filthy-rich bloodsuckers, and slumlords preying on their tenants. The press surely doesn't help my cause, always bringing its readers up to date with the latest horror stories.

Every landlord will encounter trouble with tenants, not because property owners are sadists who enjoy punishing people, but because tenants sometime act inappropriately and deserve a slap on the wrist. Despite the book's depiction of some peccadilloes and more common misdeeds, such as not paying rent or the use of foul language, I want to make it clear to my readers that I don't mean to denigrate any tenant, not even the bad ones. They all put food on my table, and without them I'd be out of business. I hope, by the time readers finish the final chapter, those who still have negative opinions of landlords will start asking themselves whether maybe, just maybe, those opinions are wrong. Landlords really are people too.

My book concentrates on a small minority of troublemakers who have made, and continue to make, my life very challenging, and sometimes, downright miserable. It's also necessary that I include my interaction with a few New York City agencies that often come between my tenants and me: The Environmental Control Board, often referred to as the ECB; the New York City Department of Health and Mental Hygiene, the New

York City Department of Buildings, The New York City Police Department, the Con Edison Electric company and the Key span gas company, now referred to as National Grid.

I believe you should get a brief look at my background so you'll understand how easy it was for me to transform from a country yokel into a street-smart cosmopolitan entrepreneur who, through extreme diligence and perseverance, immediately became adept at stumbling and fumbling throughout his career. I was born and raised in a place I call "Deadville," a small town in the Midwest where driving three miles over the speed limit runs the risk of a ticket, where a man was once arrested in his own home for playing poker for money, where the use of the word "sex" or the expression "this sucks" earns you a smack across the chops. Where a woman called 911 when she spotted a raccoon in her backyard, prompting six police officers to zoom in for the kill. When, at twenty-eight years of age, I had to ask my mother what the expression "rip off" meant.

Now everyone can plainly see that I have the credentials to succeed in any major metropolis.

One day my wife, who was sick and tired of living with me after six boring years in Deadville, issued an ultimatum.

"Either you start a new life with me in the Big Apple, or we'll go our separate ways. If you want to stay here in your honky-tonk town, go ahead, but without me."

I realized that it was going to be her way or the highway. Just my luck: the highway was closed.

CHAPTER ONE

THE FIRST PURCHASE

IN 1975 THE ECONOMY in New York was in horrible shape. Interest rates were sky high. Capital gains tax, the tax you pay when you make a profit from a real estate sale was close to 40%. Though dying to sell, this exorbitant rate discouraged most property owners from selling their buildings and buying new ones. First time buyers were waiting for a better market and construction was at a standstill. In short, the market stunk. Despite this gloomy picture I never stopped thinking about the skyscrapers I saw when we sailed into the New York Harbor. I made up my mind that, one day soon I'd buy one of them. But, before realizing my dream, I had to have more than $5,000 to my name. I didn't have a profession and I was too proud to work for anybody. Luckily, my wife was a designer and seamstress. I took advantage of this by finding a small space to rent and rounding up some dress manufacturers who hired us to sew dresses for them. For the next three and a half years, we put aside as much money as possible.

One weekend in 1979, while I was walking my dog, I saw a sign that read "Commercial building for sale. Owner will finance." The property in question was an empty building in a high-traffic area of Queens, close to our sewing factory. I decided to check it out. It wasn't a skyscraper, but I was ready to buy it, even if it was a teeny-weeny bit smaller. The owner, Mr. Comenser, told me that if I were serious about buying his building I wouldn't have to finance the purchase through a bank. He would be my mortgagee.

"I'll charge you only 11 percent interest," he said. "That's a far cry from the 16 or 17 percent the bank charges today."

What a deal! How could I pass that up? I didn't.

Thirty-five days later, shortly after the title report came back, showing that the property was free of violations and attachments, Mr. Comenser shook my hand.

"Good luck, Mr. Carlos, you are now a landlord," he said, perhaps with a touch of sarcasm.

PART I: JOHN OTTOMAN AND BELLA UGLIA

So NOW THAT I was a landlord, my first job was finding tenants. I needed one for the first floor and one for the second floor. John Ottoman had a furniture store six blocks away. His existing space was smaller than my available first floor. He asked me if he could relocate to my building. He tried convincing me that he was well established and that his customers wouldn't have to walk much farther to my store than to his. I told him that I'd think about it and get back to him in a day or two.

I questioned several shopkeepers that had stores in the same neighborhood to learn what kind of person Mr. Ottoman was and how his business was doing. All of them agreed that his store was always busy, and as far as they knew, no one had ever said a bad word about him. On the contrary, those who knew him said that he was a gem and that he had been in business there for over five years. I was convinced that he'd be okay, so I didn't hesitate to draw up a lease. I figured that if I wanted him to remain my tenant, I'd have to give him a long lease and keep the rent as low as possible. The minute he signed, I found myself on cloud nine.

Now that I had wrapped up one tenant, I was chomping at the bit to wrap up another. Three days later, I wrapped her up. Oh boy, did I wrap her up, pink ribbons and all.

Bella Uglia, an extremely unpleasant woman, became my second-floor tenant, moving in two weeks after Mr. Ottoman. She was a sewing contractor who needed more space for her business. Four dress manufacturers were steadily supplying her work, so I didn't worry that she would have a problem paying the rent.

Despite being charming and hospitable to her employees, she was the exact opposite to me. I never suspected that she was a bitch on wheels. Everyday she cursed me, always including the word *maricón* or *coño*, two dirty non-complimentary slang expressions. Once she screamed at the top of her lungs that the steps leading to the second floor were not clean enough to suit her. Another time she lambasted me for not replacing a windowpane fast enough, using every vulgar word imaginable to express her rage. When I told her that it was her responsibility to remove litter from the sidewalk in front of the door leading to her shop, she practically took my head off. In the lease it clearly stated that she was responsible to remove it. It was clear to me why her name was Uglia. She was no beauty queen. But how does Bella fit in? Bella means pretty in Spanish. I sure as hell didn't have the answer. Her hair was tinted green, which made me sick to look at, and she smelled so bad that I was tempted to buy her underarm deodorant. If that's not enough, she desperately needed an orthodontist to reverse the direction of her two remaining teeth. I was afraid that if she displayed them an angry male dog might suspect that she was not human but a fellow K-9 and not be able to restrain himself from attacking her. But then again, she'd probably win the fight. To top it off, she was terribly obese. But as long as she could squeeze through the second floor entry door to her sewing factory I could live with it. You are probably wondering why

I'm so cruel describing her in such a negative way? This woman was vicious. There was no other way to portray her.

The next two years were uneventful, but two or three months into the third year, both tenants started giving me an earful. Each of them had a different problem.

Ottoman still had eighteen months left on his lease and started complaining that his business was slacking off. He said that unless I lowered his rent, he'd have to close. I told him that that was impossible.

"But," I said, "I have a plan that can save both of us. How about I give you $15,000 right now, today, and pay the storage charges for your furniture until you find another place? Would that be acceptable?"

To my utter surprise, without even taking a minute to think, he shook my hand.

"You better believe it's acceptable. Thank you very much, sir. You're being more than generous."

I guess my training in Deadville was starting to reap rewards. But I couldn't afford to bask in glory. I was left with an empty store and had to put another ad in the paper for a new tenant. But I should have been happy. This would prove a breeze compared to what came next.

One week later, Mrs. Uglia started crying that all her suppliers had stopped giving her work. She tried finding new work but was unsuccessful. I didn't have to hear more. I knew that I'd never see another dime. I tried convincing her to face reality and stop looking for work that didn't exist and gave her two weeks to vacate. She scowled and snorted but didn't respond. I even gave her permission to put her sewing machines in the basement for a reasonable time until she found a place to move. Every time I got close to her, I had the good fortune to get a whiff of her stinky breath. Two weeks later, she refused to budge. I had no choice but to hire a lawyer and get her barking ass out.

Stanley Ouster, a partner in the firm of Ouster, Edjector, and Pushitt, listened to my tale of woe. When Ouster heard the words "sewing machines," he cautioned me that it could take more than three months to evict her. I suspected he was right but asked him to do his best to speed things up. When he asked me to describe her, I paused for a moment to think of something more precise than "mixed breed."

"Actually, she could be mistaken for an overstuffed chihuahua. If this particular description doesn't help, you may recognize her if you're fortunate enough to see her fucked-up teeth. Trust me; you'll know it's her."

Three days later, Ouster called me to his office.

"Talk to me, counselor," I said. "What do you have for me?"

"What I am about to tell you is the whole truth and nothing but the truth, so help me God."

"We're not in court," I said. "Get on with it."

"Okay. I went to her sewing shop, but she wasn't there. One of the sewing operators told me she was at a diner and would return within the hour. I had no patience to wait, so rather than stand there doing nothing, I went to the post office to buy some stamps, standing on line with sixteen other disenchanted grumblers. Just when I heard the magic word 'Next,' I spotted a woman, or something similar to a woman, fitting your description. The odds were that in a community of 200,000 people, it wasn't her, but what did I have to lose by asking? The man standing behind me held my spot and I walked over to the counter where she was fiddling with some papers. 'Are you by any chance Mrs. Uglia?' I asked. "Yeah" she said. Who wants to know?' The second she turned to face me; I got a strong whiff of her foul breath that almost knocked me off my feet. I wasn't sure if she had halitosis or some other form of disgusting hoof and mouth disease. I was close to passing out, so I shoved the five-day notice into her purse and sped out of the post office as fast as my legs could carry me. You know what, on second thought, maybe I wasn't being fair. She could have brushed her teeth that morning but simply failed to apply enough toothpaste to the brush. Wow, were you right about the teeth. What was the pedigree? I couldn't be sure. It looked like a chihuahua. Can you believe it, Mr. Carlos, that in a community this large, I'd stumble into the right canine?"

We both shed tears from laughing so hard.

Bella's super-slick lawyer, along with two bleeding-heart judges, bought her seven more months before I could finally say good riddance. I pity her new landlord.

The second floor remained empty until I found a wholesale clothing distributor. He was a good guy who always paid his rent on time, seldom complaining. No story there.

PART II: WON HUNG LOO

Won Hung loo was the first one responding to my ad for the first-floor vacancy. He was dead set on opening a Laundromat. I wasn't crazy about having a Laundromat in my building. I knew that he'd have to break up the cement floor in the basement in order to install some huge machines, plus load up the first floor with washing machines and dryers. I also knew that if he didn't pay his water bills, I'd get stuck with them. The water department doesn't care if the lease obligates the tenant to pay. Despite all these concerns, I chose to let him move in. He was such a decent guy that I ignored basic business fundamentals, giving him a huge break on the rent. Maybe I still lacked a bit of experience. Only the good lord knows why. Two weeks later, won was open for business. We lived in harmony for almost five years. You couldn't find a better tenant. He always paid his rent right on time.

But one day, out of the blue, like Ottoman, Won started to cry. They were crocodile tears. I almost cried with him.

"You no help put rent down must go. Me sorry, Mr. Carlos."

"I am sorry too, Won," I said, "but I can't do it. Times are tough and I can't make more exceptions. The only thing I can do is, if you want, try to sell the machines for you. If no one buys them, I'll help you move them to a place of your choice."

For two months, people were popping in and out, but no one bought a thing. I was temporarily stuck with a fully equipped Laundromat, stuffed with fifteen washers and dryers, two coin machines, two soap dispensers, a jukebox, a candy machine, a sandwich machine, a soda machine, a rocking horse, and a humongous wooden duck that quacked every time you bumped into the damn thing. Finally, I gave up and called a scrap yard. The good news was that they came. The bad news was that they didn't pay me a nickel for the stuff. I had to pay them, and it sure as hell wasn't cheap. Now, you think Won and I were divorced? Wrong. The following story explains how the marriage continued.

CHAPTER TWO

THE WATER METER

THE DAY THAT THE tenant finishes his lease, he's obligated to order a special water meter reading so the new tenant doesn't get stuck with his bills. Woncomplied and I witnessed the reading. The following day I closed the store. I tried to find a new tenant but was unsuccessful. The store remained closed for two and a half years.

Two years later, I received a notice from the post office that they had a letter for me.

The letter said that if I didn't pay the New York City Water Board charges of $38,000, plus penalty and interest, I could lose my building in a lien sale. I had no clue what this was all about. I had been there when they read the meter and I was positive that Won had paid the bill. I was also positive that he didn't bounce the check. Mad as hell, I went to the water department for answers. Miss Oreo greeted me, a young lass who held a glass of tea in one hand and had cookie crumbs stuck to her bottom lip. She informed me that the water department sent eight bills to both the business address and the home of the tenant, but no one responded.

"So, Mr. Carlos, if you don't want to lose your building, pay up! You're a rich guy. You can always appeal later."

"Wonderful," I said. "But first show me the bills you're referring to."

As I suspected, the bills were all based on estimated readings. I asked her why they had waited so long to threaten me.

"Maybe," I said, "if you'd had the marshal break down the door to read the meter six months ago, you'd have discovered that I owe you $50,000, not $38,000."

I could see on her face that she wasn't thrilled with my comments. But then she began grinning from ear to ear.

Cookie crumbs still stuck to her bottom lip, she said, "Mister, you don't have a choice. Pay the money now. Like I said before, you can always appeal."

I sensed from her tone of voice that she enjoyed torturing me. I was dying to smack the breadcrumbs off her lip with a wet dishrag, but where could I find a dishrag in this dump? There was no way out. I was a dead duck. I couldn't leave her desk without telling her a couple things.

"My dear Miss Oreo, do you realize that if someone had notified me a lot earlier, I wouldn't have to stand here looking at that stupid cookie crumb on your bottom lip, fighting to restrain myself from whacking it off with a dishrag? You're lucky that I probably wouldn't find one in this dump."

"Good-bye sir," she said, "and close the door behind you."

The following day, I returned with a certified check for $38,000, including penalties and interest. While passing Cookie Lips on the way to the cashier, I couldn't resist telling her something that you'd never hear on prime time television. I didn't give two hoots in hell who heard me. As soon as I returned home, I demanded a water meter reading to prove, beyond a doubt, there was no water usage from the time Won left, up to the present day. Once again, I witnessed the water meter reading. As I suspected, the reading was the same as the previous one. Armed with proof, I composed a two-page letter to the water board, which explained how they had screwed me and demanded all my money back. I warned them that if they dilly-dallied too long, my lawyer would sue their ass from here to Timbuktu and back.

My letter obviously scared them to death because they rebated me the $38,000 six months later not a year later, which is usually how long you might have to wait in cases like this. Now you must be asking yourself, what happened here? I'm not sure myself, but here are a few possibilities. Either some idiot in the water department lost the paper containing the final meter reading or forgot to enter it into the system. The bottom line is the water department didn't care that the Laundromat was closed and not using water. Later, I learned that Won moved out of state without leaving a forwarding address. All the water bills mailed to his home probably found their way to the garbage. What happened to the bills mailed to the Laundromat? I don't have a clue. I never saw any water bills there, and as far as I know, neither did anyone else. If I was smart, I could have received permission from Yan to have the water company mail me copies of his bills. This way, the whole episode might have been avoided. It seems that I just didn't want to learn that in order to survive, a landlord must anticipate every eventuality. A paranoid personality helps. You simply can't trust anyone, especially city agencies.

A couple weeks later, I rented the space to a South American restaurateur. I am happy to say, he's still with me. No story here.

CHAPTER THREE

BROOKLYN

IN THE MID-EIGHTIES I purchased a building in Brooklyn. It was a mixed-use three-story structure with one thousand square feet of empty first-floor commercial space, four attached garages, one occupied apartment on the second floor, and two occupied apartments on the third floor. Like my first building in Queens, the owner became my mortgagee. That was the good news. The bad news was that two of my three inherited residential tenants were rotten to the core. But I'll return to them later. I'll begin with the commercial tenants.

PART I: JIMBO

MY FIRST TASK WAS finding a commercial tenant for the first floor. I had no idea how hard that would be. Three weeks later, I found Jimbo Tatala or maybe he found me, I don't remember. He told me that he'd be using the space for a social club. He was a cocky young punk with rings in his ears, nose, bottom lip, tongue, and who knows where else. He had tattoos on his forearms, cheeks, palms of his hands, and who knows where else. He was wearing cowboy boots and a straw hat that was at least one size too big. His baggy pants were slipping below his waist, making me curious to know if he had more unique artistry on his rump. I couldn't wait to peek. Sorry folks, I can't, in good conscience, print what I saw. It definitely wasn't a Claude Monet or Edgar Degas tattooed on his butt cheeks, but something else, something absolutely disgusting, definitely not fit for print.

I asked Jimbo some routine questions like "On which planet were you conceived? Did your mother, after seeing you the first time, consider returning you to sender?" I'm just joking. After lengthy pondering, I changed my mind about calling Dun and Bradstreet for a credit rating. There was a good chance he wasn't in their files. But you never know. He could have been an eccentric millionaire in disguise. Jimbo said that his social club would contain only a few card tables, a jukebox, a few pinball machines and a mini-bar to serve beer and soft drinks, but no liquor. I agreed to rent the place to him, under the condition that he wouldn't engage in heavy-stakes gambling or allow ladies of the evening to frequent his club. I didn't bother warning him to obey city codes and regulations because he probably wouldn't have known what the hell I was talking about. But I did insist that he obtain a beer license and permit to have a social club. A month later, he showed me proof of compliance. After we both signed the lease, he handed me a heavy leather pouch containing two month's rent as security and the first month's rent, all in quarters. I asked him if he'd please give me green instead.

"No," he said. "That would be a big pain in my ass."

I guessed if it was a big pain in my ass, it didn't matter. I didn't want to lose him, so I kept my mouth shut. For the next two months, the quarters kept coming. But it didn't bother me that much. I had plenty of change to feed parking meters. About three or four months later, people in the neighborhood started screaming about excessive noise emanating from the club. I played deaf for a while, but when I heard the police had been there more than once, I couldn't continue ignoring the complaints. I drove over to see what was going on. Guess what?

Jimbo had flown the coop. I heard rumors that the day before, the cops had arrested him for selling drugs.

PART II: THE MAJOR

I WAS HAPPY TO be rid of him, but unhappy too. I was sure it would take me just as long to find a new tenant as it had taken to find Jimbo. At that point, I didn't care if my next tenant had safety pins in his ass, just so he didn't have any pornographic tattoos on his body. I was in no position to be fussy. I got lucky. I found someone in less than a week. They called him the Major, although he sure as hell wasn't Army material. He dressed in fatigues and cowboy boots and he was bald as a cue ball. I don't know why, but I liked the guy from the start. He told me he was renting a social club in a building three blocks away, and the owner of the building was selling it to his cousin. The Major didn't have a lease on his current property, so he knew that his cousin could kick him out at any time. My spot was perfect for him.

Compared to Jimbo, he was a duke, not a Major. He was heavily adorned with jewelry, but thank the lord, nothing was stapled to his lips, nose, or tongue. I was equally grateful that he wore his pants above the waist.

The Major paid his rent (in dollar bills) on the first or second of every month. I knew he was selling numbers, but I didn't care, as long as he wasn't involved in pornography, especially child pornography, or heavy gambling and drugs. In the Major's club there were always a few tough looking guys wearing Hell's Angel Jackets and stomping boots. I was friendly with all of them. I didn't need enemies. Two weeks after the Major moved in, I had already established a warm relationship with him and everyone else in the place. I considered inviting the major and all the club members and guests to dinner, and afterward, taking them to the opera to hear Lily Pons sing *Aida* in her inimitable style. But when I gave it a second thought,

I changed my mind. What if my wife was unhappy about it? Three years passed without incident, but then I started hearing rumors that the cops were in the Major's club at least once a week. One of the neighbors told me, though she didn't have proof, that someone had been shot inside the club and whisked away in a van. The Major knew he could trust me to keep my mouth shut. But this was the last straw. A possible murder, cops, numbers, and maybe something else I wasn't aware of. The Major had to go. When I told him that I wasn't looking to get arrested for criminal complicity, he showed complete understanding and agreed to find another spot. Two weeks later we shook hands and hugged one another. Just before he left, he handed me a piece of paper with his home address in Puerto Rico and his telephone number. It was an easy job cleaning out his old space. But this time, instead of looking for a new tenant, I kept it closed until I sold the building.

PART III: MRS. PUTALA

MRS. PUTALA, ONE OF my two residential tenants on the third floor, was a slovenly, mean bitch living with her two teenage sons. I could stand on my head and expectorate three times, but it wouldn't help me to think of anything nice to say about her. Each son had a different father and I'm positive that neither of them would have hesitated to punch me out. The rumor was that both sons were repeatedly in trouble with the law.

I recall a time when I was walking toward the building to collect rent and noticed a woman leaning out of the window on the third floor. As I drew closer, I saw that it was Mrs. Putala. When she recognized me she started screaming at the top of her lungs.

"Here comes the fucking devil," she shouted.

Needless to say, I was somewhat distraught. After her charming description of me, I made sure to lower my head the rest of the way to the building where she resided. I was fortunate that some religious fanatic living in the neighborhood who hated Satan with a passion didn't hear her lovely voice and then smash my head in with a frying pan before I reached the front door. Once I was inside the building, I couldn't climb the stairs fast enough to give her a piece of my mind. When she opened the door to greet me, she was clad in a flimsy, wrinkled bathrobe with grease spots splattered all over it.

"What do you want, bloodsucker?" she asked. "It's only the sixth of the month."

I politely reminded her Royal Highness that the rent was due on the first, and she hadn't paid. Her teeth were so rotten that I wanted to suggest knocking them out to save her money on her dental bills. I asked her in a meek tone of voice when she could pay.

"Come back around the 25th and we'll see."

I nodded, showing my compassion and complete understanding. Why was I such a coward? To me it was obvious. If I asked her for the rent like a man, she never would have paid me. For the next three months she paid me promptly on the 27th or 28th of the month—very late. Each payment was laced with venom.

In the beginning of the fourth month, one of the two fathers of her children popped in for a visit. He proceeded to beat the living crap out of Mrs. Putala. When delinquent son #1 heard his mother shrieking like a pig, he rushed out of his bedroom into the living room and saw her lying on the floor, writhing in pain. She was bleeding profusely from the nose. The father had disappeared. #1 son rounded up his two delinquent brothers who were sleeping in the back bedrooms. They zoomed out of the building together on a search-and-destroy mission. Mrs. Putala was wheeled out to an ambulance. I was sure that after the sons found her assailant, they'd pummel him to death and dump him in an alley someplace. I was also sure that they'd never risk arrest by returning home. Someone in the neighborhood told me that the mother would be in the hospital for at least six months. I didn't stand on ceremony; I changed the locks the same day.

PART IV: MRS. PRIZE

Mrs. Prize lived in my second-floor apartment. She was a halfway-decent-looking woman; Finally, I was able to interrupt a miserable trend of ugliness. She lived with a beer-guzzling boyfriend and her two pregnant teenage daughters. The entire family was on welfare and food stamps. That made me suspect the situation would turn a bit sour. I was wrong; it turned catastrophic. Three months after I purchased the building, she stopped paying rent. I don't know why I waited six weeks before starting a nonpayment action. I guess you can chalk it up to compassion.

I hated the Brooklyn landlord-tenant court, but what choice did I have, other than letting her stay in the apartment for free? My attorney, Mr. Zilch, Mrs. Prize, and I soon stood before the Honorable Judge Drizzling. The judge was a slovenly shrimp, no more than five feet four inches tall with an arrogant, offensive manner, by the way. He was constantly wiping snot from his nose and saliva from his chin.

His first question was directed to Mrs. Prize. "Do you have an attorney, madam?"

She looked puzzled.

The judge rephrased the question. "Do you have a lawyer?"

"No, senor" she said.

"I am sorry, people," the judge, announced. "I will not continue this case unless the defendant also has council. Bailiff, explain to her that she must bring an attorney with her the next time she comes to court." "Am I right in saying madam that you barely speak English?"

"Si, your honor."

"Fine," the judge said. "We will meet back here in sixty days."

I felt like punching the judge in the mouth, but it wasn't worth it. I knew that eventually he'd drown in his own spit.

Sixty days later, Mr. Zilch, Mrs. Prize and I, once again, stood before Judge Drizzling.

The Judge directed his first question to Mrs. Prize. "Where is your lawyer, madam?"

"Don't have one," she answered.

The judge, with a supercilious smirk on his face, looked me straight in the eyes and said, "You all heard her. She doesn't have one. We will provide the defendant with a public defender and meet back here in two weeks. Case adjourned."

As you probably guessed, I kept my big mouth shut.

Two weeks later, Mrs. Prize, Mr. Zilch, Mr. Linguist (the public defender), and the victim, Mr. Carlos, stood before the honorable Judge Drizzling.

The judge directed his first question to Mr. Linguist. "I trust, sir, that your command of the Spanish language is sufficient so we can finally move on."

"Your honor, I will do my best."

"Your best, sir?"

At this point, the 60 percent of water in my body was quickly rising to 212 degrees Fahrenheit. My lawyer advised me not to do anything that might require the judge to change his name from Drizzling to Gusher. The judge noticed I was somewhat distraught, so he waited until I regained my composure. Then he continued.

"You realize, madam," he said, "we can't continue unless you understand everything that is said here." I noticed the public defender whispering something in her ear. Maybe he was interpreting what the judge told her. My patience was wearing thin.

Mrs. Prize blurted something out. "Your honor, my mother is sick in my country and I have to visit her soon."

"Oh," the judge said with a deadpan expression on his face, "I see that you can speak English. Let's proceed."

My lawyer smiled at me but I didn't return the smile.

"Madam." "How can you fly to Puerto Rico if you don't have money for the rent? Doesn't welfare provide you with rent money?" the judge asked.

"Yes, your honor, but it isn't enough."

Judge Drizzling, without saying a word, looked me straight in the eyes. This time with a smile, not a smirk, thank God. Then he turned back to face Mrs. Prize, shocking me with his next comment.

"Don't let welfare find out that you are using the rent money for other things."

My impotent lawyer and I looked at each other in disbelief. I started wondering if this judge might be a phony who killed the real one and took his place.

The alleged judge asked everyone to remain silent. "I have a proposal that I hope each side will accept." He said.

I waited with baited breath.

"Would both sides agree to sign a stipulation that the defendant can remain in the apartment for an additional forty-five days? This should give her sufficient time to find a more affordable apartment. But, if she doesn't move by that time, she will have to pay the landlord use and occupancy."

Mr. Zilch looked at me. "Take the offer. If you don't, you'll never get her out."

I knew Zilch was right. "It's okay with me, your honor," I said.

Now it was up to Mrs. Prize to agree. Only the good lord above could help me if she didn't. Who knows? Maybe if she didn't accept the terms, the judge would have let her stay another six months. I chewed my nails as I awaited her answer.

Finally the suspense was over. "Yes, your honor. I accept the terms. I want to thank you for being so fair, impartial, and compassionate."

For a second, I thought she had been moonlighting as an English teacher. You never know these days. Exactly forty-four days later, my cupcake vacated the apartment. How much did this whole episode cost me? It's too painful to think about. I'm better off putting it behind me.

PART V: LONGALUX AND GRIME

MY OTHER THIRD-FLOOR TENANT, Mr. Longalux, was an African-American who stood at least six feet five inches tall. We first met in a real estate office. His broker told me that Mr. Longalux had been forced to vacate his Harlem apartment because the owner was selling the building, and Longalux was looking for an apartment to rent closer to his auto parts store. The broker added that Mr. Longalux would be living with his girlfriend Alotta Grime and her thirteen-year-old daughter.

Quite frankly, I was scared stiff of Mr. Longalux, but I didn't want a discrimination lawsuit. With all my resolve, I stood directly in front of him, steadfastly maintaining eye contact. It was difficult to say the least. I am only five-seven and my neck was killing me.

Trying not to stutter, I courageously gave him advance warning of my ground rules. "Sir, I want to make it perfectly clear that I will not tolerate late rent payments or sloppy living conditions. If you are right by me, I'll be right by you." I reached out to shake his hand, praying that he'd have mercy on me and not squeeze too hard.

But the lord was busy with more pressing problems. Longalux squeezed my hand so firmly that I couldn't decide which was worse, the pain in my neck or the pain in my hand. He seemed to respect me for not flinching as he squeezed my hand.

"You don't have to worry, sir," he said. "I will be your best tenant." Again, possibly due to lack of experience, I neglected to request meeting his girl friend and her daughter. This oversight proved disastrous. Because Mr. Longalux had his own business, the rent wasn't an issue. But you'll soon see that proved to be another crucial mistake. He paid me one-month security and one month rent. We shook hands again, but this time, I squeezed as hard as I could, causing tears to form in both my eyes. I made damn sure not to flinch.

On the first day of the following month I met Alotta Grime. She opened her apartment door, greeting me with a menacing look. She was scary to behold and for a second I thought she was going to hit me with an ax. Behind her, I saw dirty, smelly clothes scattered over the living room floor and a naked girl running through the hallway. Alotta reluctantly let me in. Without asking her permission, I went from room to room to see whatever there was to see. The kitchen was a mess. It looked like the garbage hadn't been removed for a week. Dirty pots and pans were piled up in the sink. Spoiled meat on the Formica counter was drawing flies, and the stovetop was covered with grease. In each room, the floors were filthy, sadly in need of mopping.

Both bedroom carpets were covered with used toilet paper, stinking from urine. I was ready to puke, but told myself to wait until the rent money was in my hands. I watched her wiggle her fat behind while she walked back to the rear bedroom to retrieve my rent. Five minutes later she returned empty-handed.

"My boyfriend didn't leave the money," she said.

I was furious. I had to wait for the rent inside a stinky, rotten apartment, and now I'd have to walk out with nothing?

"Listen, gorgeous, you better get your act together and get me my money. I don't care if you have to rob a bank. Just get me my money," I said sternly.

She wasn't a bit scared, telling me to calm my ass down. "I'll call my boyfriend," she said. He's probably got your damn rent." After speaking with him for a couple of minutes, she passed me the phone. "Here, he wants to talk to you."

Mr. Longalux apologized profusely. "I am very sorry, sir," he said. "This will never happen again. From now on, I'll be your best tenant. Come to my office. I'll pay you in cash."

"Okay," I said. "But this will be the last time I'll do this."

I drove to his office, praying I wouldn't catch any red lights. I was lucky to find a parking spot directly across the street from his store. Longalux paid me right away, apologizing once again for the inconvenience. Then he told me the last thing in the world I wanted to hear.

"I have to go away on business for a month or two, but don't worry. Alotta will pay you the rent while I'm gone."

What miserable luck, I thought to myself, *but what choice did I have?* Oh, I forgot to mention a tiny detail. Sneaky Mr. Longalux had already sold his business and bought two one-way airline tickets to Brazil. He bought one ticket for his mistress, who I never knew existed, and one for himself. I was now stuck with Longalux's daughter and Alotta Grime as tenants. My first instinct was to jump off the Brooklyn Bridge and end it there. On the first of the following month, I knocked on Alotta's door, but there was nobody home. I returned to my car, feeling like a total failure. Two days later, I received a certified letter from Alotta's lawyer. The letter told me that I had violated the certificate of occupancy by adding a third apartment to the floor. But I hadn't added anything. The guy who sold me the building did. In this neighborhood several landlords were guilty of doing the same thing, but no one was ever caught. I knew the conversion was illegal from day one. The certificate of occupancy clearly stated that it was a two-family apartment building with one store. If somebody squealed to the building department and the other tenants in the building got wind of it, they could have lived there rent-free. As a result, many landlords in all five boroughs had lost their buildings in foreclosures.

PART VI: THE EJECTMENT ACTION

WHEN BUSTED FOR AN illegal conversion, in addition to dismantling the illegal apartment, the landlord must endure a lengthy trial, which, in my case, lasted fourteen months and you can forget about getting any rent. The tenant does not have to pay the landlord a nickel. And get this, if any other tenants in the building become aware of this scenario, they also can live rent-free. I was lucky. I only had Alotta on my plate. At the time, the law stipulated that if the building was assessed for $25,000 or less, the case, referred to, as an "ejectment action" would be heard in civil court. If the value were assessed at one penny more than $25,000, the case would go to the New York City

Supreme Court. For a change, I was lucky. My case stayed in civil court. Even though the fines in civil court are far less than they are in Supreme Court, they were high enough to cause me financial stress. What Mrs. Grime put me through the next fourteen months, neither Satan nor any of his underlings could have orchestrated more effectively.

During the trial, the judge allowed me to ask questions. My lawyer never stopped me. He knew that no matter what I said it wouldn't have any bearing on the judge's verdict. This was an open-and-shut case. In an ejectment action, there is never an innocent verdict. The whole trial was a waste of time. I asked the Judge why Mrs. Grime was allowed to live in an apartment that had rotten food on top of all the kitchen counters and garbage scattered all over?

My question must have irritated him because he cut me off and replied, "You have council representing you. Let him do what you retained him to do. Why didn't you call the health department before? You are the landlord. You are responsible for everything that happens in your building"

"Can I answer that, your honor?"

"Go ahead" the judge replied.

"On other occasions, I did call the health department but they never did a thing, probably thinking I made up the story to get rid of her."

"Listen sir," the judge interrupted. "I have been very patient with you, but I can't help you. It is out of my jurisdiction. And I have one piece of advice for you: Don't bother starting a nonpayment action. First, you have to finish with me."

My lawyer remained silent. He knew there was nothing he could do to help me. I was lucky that my other two tenants were unaware of my predicament. The trial, between loss of rent and legal fees, cost me over $18,000. Not only was I hurt financially, but also I had to witness the victorious smile on Alotta Grime's miserable face. The same day the trial was over I hired a new lawyer for a thirty-day non-payment action. I guess she couldn't pay her lawyer because she took off before the thirty days were up. It took several years to erase this ordeal from my mind. Fortunately, Alotta Grime's replacement was a gem. I only wish that I had ten more like her. No story there.

PART VII: THE PAYNE FAMILY

Mrs. Payne, the tenant on the third floor who replaced Mrs. Prize, was a harmless young lady living with her husband and their two daughters. Mr. Payne had previously lived in the Bronx and needed an apartment closer to his job site.

During the second month of their tenancy, I received a phone call in the middle of the night. It was Mrs. Payne. She was talking so fast that I could hardly understand her. "*Venga, venga señor*. It's my husband. You have to find me another apartment. I can't live here any longer."

She was calling me at two in the morning; the situation had to be urgent. I sped there as fast as possible. The minute she opened the door, I saw Mr. Payne sprawled on the couch. His face looked like it had gone through a meat grinder. His wife and their two daughters were crying hysterically, the kids were helping their mother apply ice packs to his cheeks. The scene was heartbreaking.

"*Señora*, what happened?" I asked.

She told me that her husband had been on his way home from his night job, and the second he got off the train, two animals jumped him. They repeatedly kicked him in the ribs, took all his money, and when he struggled to get up, threw him back down and kicked him some more. "I don't know how he was able to walk home," she said.

"I don't know either," I said. Feeling her pain, I reached into my pocket and handed her ten $100 bills, asking her if it was enough to tide her over until her husband was on his feet.

She hugged and kissed me over and over again on the cheek, thanking me several times, but I told her thanks weren't necessary. I then asked her if she wanted me to take her husband to the hospital.

"No need," she answered. "He'll be okay."

I promised to do my best to find her an apartment, and if worse came to worse, let her stay in one of my empty ones until her husband was on his feet. Two weeks later she took her husband and daughters to move in with some relatives.

CHAPTER FOUR

THE GARAGE

THE FOLLOWING STORY ILLUSTRATES why you don't rent a garage to anyone unless you investigate him or her thoroughly. It's important to know if a person is known around the neighborhood, if he or she has been arrested, and maybe most important, did he or she rent another garage nearby and stiff the landlord on the rent? But for me, a handshake, photo ID, and present address were sufficient proof at that time. C'mon, what could possibly go wrong with a tenant who pays a lousy $50 a month for a lousy garage?

From day one, Barry Contrary was a royal pain in my butt. Without permission, he set up inside my garage a café, selling beer, hamburgers, hot dogs, and minute steaks. People were standing in line, drooling in anticipation. Why not? His overhead was minimal, so he could sell cheap, and the nearest eatery was six blocks away. The smoke from the barbecue units stunk up the garage so badly that sometimes you couldn't breathe. But who was going to complain? Even the police stopped there for coffee and a sandwich. But the certificate of occupancy stated clearly that garages could be used only for parking vehicles.

Three weeks later, when I couldn't take it any more, I called the fire department, police department, ECB, and health department to boot him out. Except for the fire department, they all told me that the beef with my tenant was a landlord-tenant matter, and if I wanted him out, I'd have to go through proper channels. It looked like I was a dead duck and would have to accept my fate. What did the fire department say? They told me that they had passed by the garage on several occasions and didn't consider it a fire hazard. Of course it's not a fire hazard. How could it be? Firemen were dining there and supplied napkins as well.

Around seven-thirty in the morning, a couple days after I called the agencies above, I was passing by the garage and noticed that the gate was partially open. I peeked inside and saw a car that looked like a Rolls Royce, but I couldn't make out the license plates. I was sure that Barry Contrary wasn't rich enough to drive such an expensive car. The Rolls was most likely stolen! A couple days before, I had been talking to Barry in the garage and didn't see any cars, so he or a friend had probably just brought it there.

I was certain that the police would be eager to hear about what I suspected of being a stolen car. But a desk sergeant heard my story and brushed me off.

"What proof do you have that the car was stolen? Did you see the plates?"

"No, officer," I answered.

"Well, unless you can prove to me that the car was stolen, we are not going to come down there and waste our time."

I was really pissed off and back to square one, stuck with a garage stinking to high heaven, filled with pots and pans, a greasy barbecue unit, scattered tools, and a brand-new Rolls-Royce. But a few days later, while examining some graffiti on the building next to the garages, I saw a police car pull up to the curb in front of the corner deli.

One of the two officers went into the store. The other one remained in the car. Just for the hell of it, I walked over to the car and asked the officer if he had any suggestions about how I could remove a stolen car from my garage. He was from the same precinct as the desk sergeant that I spoke to previously, but he didn't know anything about our conversation.

"I know a guy who has a heavy-duty lock cutter, and he might have a tow truck guy for you. If he doesn't, you'll have to find one on your own. Write down this number and tell him I talked to you. Make sure you set it up so the tow truck guy and my friend get there at the same time. And one more thing, if you ever open your mouth about me telling you this, I'll know where to find you. Do you understand me?"

His partner returned to the car. My new cop friend gave me a wink. I stood there at the curbside, stunned. Was this real? Did this really happen? I learned one thing that day. Policemen are no different than the rest of us. Some are good, some are bad, and some go the extra mile. I did exactly what the officer told me to do. Excuse me, "suggested" that I do. His lock cutter friend didn't have a tow truck man for me, so I had to look for one myself. I found a tow truck company in the yellow pages and waited outside their garage until the drivers finished their shift.

I stopped one of them as he headed out for the day. "Are you ready to make five hundred bucks for a couple hours work?" I asked.

His face lit up. "Yeah, man. What do I gotta do?"

I told him everything that he needed to know and then he said "I need Ken to come too."

"That's okay with me," I said. "But $500 is my limit. Take it or leave it."

"For $600, we'll do it. Not a penny less," he said.

I needed him more than he needed me. He had me by the ying-yangs. "Okay," I said. "I'll meet you one block from the garage on the corner of Smith Street and Adams at two a.m. sharp. My lock cutter will be there at the same time. You know how to get there, right?"

"Yeah man, I'll see you there."

I felt like a criminal on his first auto heist. But maybe I was being too hard on myself. A policeman had practically authorized it. I arrived before the appointed time to make sure there weren't any snoops around. The tow truck drivers and the lock cutter showed up right on time. Jerry Puller and Tommy Lockett remained in their truck while Buster Snippitt (the lock cutter) and I walked to the garage. I kept looking around to see if anybody was watching us. Just as Buster was ready to snip open the lock, a black cat leaped in front of us, scaring us half to death. This caused Buster to drop the cutter and inadvertently kick it into the middle of the street. My mother once told me that a black cat is a sign of bad luck. I prayed to the lord to postpone it for at least a day or two. Buster retrieved the cutter and snipped away until the lock was open. I went back to the tow truck to get Jerry and Tommy. I climbed into their truck, cautioning them to drive extra slowly. They removed the car from the garage in less than five minutes. I suggested that they dump the car near a chop shop in Ozone Park. They were already planning to do so. I reminded all three of my partners in crime to keep their mouths shut.

Jerry said, "Don't worry, we ain't ready to go to the can."

I wondered if he should have said, "go to the can again."

To kill time, I stayed in a diner until thirty minutes before Barry Contrary usually opened the garage. As I was parking my car around the corner, I heard loud screaming coming from the area of the garage. It was Barry Contrary.

"Oh my god, some motherfucker stole my car," he shouted. "I'll get that son of a bitch if it's the last thing I do."

"You better call the police," I said, trying to show compassion.

"I ain't calling no cops. They ain't worth the powder to blow 'em to hell."

"So what are you going to do?" I asked.

"I'll take care of it myself. I'll take two guys I know from Jersey, and when I find him, I'll whip his ass so bad that even his mother won't recognize him."

"I don't blame you," I said. I asked him if he suspected his co-workers in the garage.

"No way," he said. "I know these guys for ten years. They'd never do nuttin' to hurt me."

Suddenly I had an idea that would change his mind. I simply had to convince him that he was wrong and that the culprit, or culprits, was one or more of his coworkers.

"Barry," I said. "You told me that you just bought the car, so other than your buddies that are here with you, who the hell else could know it was here, unless you told somebody? It has to be one of your people."

He stood for a minute, rubbing his chin. "You're right, brother. Who else could it be?"

So Barry rounded up his Jersey boys and, like the Putala boys, went on a search-and-destroy mission. I changed the locks and kept the garage closed. There was no reason to worry about Barry returning, since the cops would want to arrest him for either murder, assault, auto theft, or all three. After that, I was scared to rent a garage, even to a priest. But you will soon see how fast my trepidation vanished.

CHAPTER FIVE

THE VISIONARIES

THREE WEEKS AFTER MOVING in, without my knowledge, Tony Pimponi and his beautiful wife Rita, both gainfully employed in a supermarket, decided to supplement their income by opening a house of ill repute in my apartment building. They were very discreet. I had no reason to suspect anything until one day when an anonymous caller from the building next door called me at home, concerned there was some hanky-panky going on in one of my apartments. He didn't have proof, but suggested that I look into it.

The following night I knocked on the Pimponis' door. A young man wearing pajamas greeted me and, before I could say a word, asked what I wanted at such a late hour.

"I'm sorry to intrude on your privacy, sir, but somebody in the neighborhood is complaining about excessive noise coming from here."

Before he answered, I noticed a scantily clad young lady in her early twenties sitting alone at a table near the kitchen. I pretended not to notice.

"I don't know what you mean sir," the young man said. "Someone is lying to you."

There was nothing left for me to try, so I apologized for intruding and left. I was not aware that one week earlier the police had raided the apartment, arresting three girls. The two weeks after my visit passed without incident. But the police then raided the apartment again, arresting more girls. Neither the police nor any of the tenants in the building informed me about the raids. I can understand why the tenants played dumb. They were simply afraid to get involved. But why did the police fail to inform me? It's my building. I have a right to know. How could they assume that I knew anything?

The answer is simple. After two raids, the cops feel that the landlord should know what's happening right under his nose, and suspect that the landlord may be in cahoots with the prostitutes. After a third raid, they have no doubt. This is one of the reasons the police higher-ups in Manhattan instituted the three-strikes-and-you're-out program. I'm not sure that this program includes drugs. After a third raid, the police department obtains a court order to padlock the apartment and post a notice on the door barring entrance. Along with the notice, the police affix to the door a fifty-six page summons and complaint reading. They mail a copy to the landlord's home, and possibly to the homes of all three John Does, if they have homes. The three-strike system makes sense on paper, but like many other laws, is impractical. The police were stubbornly convinced that I knew there were prostitutes living in the apartment. But how could I have known if none of the other tenants told me that they saw streams of men and women entering and exiting the building at all hours of the night? I didn't sleep there.

A landlord accused of renting to prostitutes is at the mercy of the court. He can't remove the locks, or even think about re renting the apartment until a judge gives the okay. Getting a court date can take weeks. The trial is cut-and-dry. The landlord pays a stiff penalty, and the judge lambastes him from pillar to post. If the landlord finds a new tenant, he must bring a new lease to the police department for approval. In my case, it was a waste of time. The local cops never looked at the lease. But to keep my nose clean, I politely asked one of the officers if my new prospective tenant had a criminal record. The officer refused to tell me, stating it was privileged information.

"So I came to the station house in good faith and you send me away with nothing," I said.

He told me the same thing that I've heard a thousand times before. "You're the landlord. Monitor your building more efficiently."

What's the moral of this story? There are three. One: Develop extra-sensory perception. Two: Ask your prospective tenant two million questions instead of one million. And three: BE LUCKY.

CHAPTER SIX

KEY STORY#1

KEYS MIGHT SEEM LIKE a boring subject for a story, but these stories are quite eventful. Remember my garage tenant Mr. Contrary and how much trouble I had getting him out? Remember how I unequivocally promised myself that I would never rent another garage to anybody for as long as I live? I guess cotton was stuffed in my ears, because I decided to rent the garage next to the one Barry Contrary rented. Because I had learned a valuable lesson from that earlier rental, I was prepared to ask the right questions to any prospective garage tenants.

My first question to Mr. Angel Keyclutz, my new garage renter was "Can you afford to pay $50 a month?" My second question was "Where do you live?" My last question was "What's your phone number?" I'd call this thorough questioning. Wouldn't you?

Angel was comfortably settled in his garage space for three months, always paying his rent on time. But in the wee hours of one morning, my home phone rang. It was Angel Keyclutz.

"Please Mr. Carlos, you have to help me. I lost my keys to the garage and I have to get my cab out. This is my living. You must have a copy of my key. I am desperate, Mr. Carlos. Please come right away."

Did I have a choice? The poor bastard needed to drive the cab to feed his family. I told him that I'd be right over with the key. The minute I arrived, he hugged me. When he attempted to shake my hand, I gave him my pinkie instead. I didn't need another Longalux experience.

"You saved me," he said. It felt so good to be appreciated. I wiped the tears and cobwebs from my eyes and reached in my pocket for his garage key. I ran my fingers through all of my many keys, but couldn't find the one that would open his garage. Frantically, I looked in my other pockets with the same results.

Angel started getting nervous and irritable. "You said that you have the key," he hollered. "Where is the mother effing key?"

This outburst alone told me he came from better stock than Barry Contrary. This guy was able to express his rage without using profanity. After tearing my car apart and still coming up empty, I returned to face the music.

"I'm terribly sorry, Sir, I must have lost the key."

Tears began running down his cheeks, but before he started climbing the walls out of frustration, I told him that I'd call an emergency locksmith. This quieted him down a bit. But let's face it, we were nothing but two keyless and clueless morons yawning in the moonlight and twiddling their thumbs, anxiously awaiting their salvation. Two hours later, Jimmy Prier from the company, Prier, Prysum, and Masters, locksmiths extraordinaire, showed up. A fifteen-minute job became a thirty-minute job. I should never have showed them how desperate I was. Keyclutz looked like he was going to faint. He probably thought I was going to demand that he pay the entire bill.

"Don't worry, Angel," I said. "I take full responsibility."

He sighed in relief. Finally, Jimmy finished drilling open the padlock and pushing up the garage door. I asked why he hadn't just snipped off the damn lock.

His answer: "That's amateurish."

After this entire hullabaloo, Angel had forgotten to bring his keys for the cab. To top it off, the drillers fucked up too, bringing the wrong padlocks for the garage gate. I closed the garage gate and drove to a hardware store, bringing back the right ones. I had to wait almost an hour until Angel returned with his keys. He was mumbling something under his breath, probably counting how much money he lost for the day. Maybe I should have counted along with him. I gave him the new heavy-duty locks plus two sets of keys and told him that if he lost the keys again, he was on his own. As we parted, Angel refused to shake my hand. I wonder why that didn't bother me?

CHAPTER SEVEN

THE STEEMHEDS

ONE DAY I WAS sixty miles north of Queens at a convention when I suddenly remembered that I had forgotten to leave my super the copies of the original key for apartment 2D. I was under the impression that the new tenants, the Steemhed family, would move into that apartment the following morning around eleven o'clock a.m. I had the original key, so to play it safe, in case the duplicate copies didn't work, I mailed the original by overnight express, to be sure that my super would get it before they arrived.

I had no idea that a moving van was already parked in front of my building and that the new tenants had already piled up their furniture on the second floor in such a way that no one could pass. It was minus-10 degrees outside, and felt the same inside. The Steemhead family had parked their butts on the damp freezing tile floor directly in front of apartment 2D for three hours, constantly wiggling in discomfort, until the locksmith, Mr. Sunheprie, finally showed up to change the key cylinder. At nine-thirty a.m. the following morning I was relieved to hear from my super that he had gotten the key, but the phone connection was terrible so I couldn't hear what else he was trying to tell me. It's a good thing I didn't, or I might have had a heart attack.

The minute the Steemheds gained entry, Mr. Steemheds began cursing for all to hear. He promised to drill the owner, meaning me, a brand-new orifice in a spot where the sun doesn't shine. Among Mr. Steemhed's personal effects was a toolbox with a drill inside, so it's quite possible that he meant what he said. After I returned and heard the whole story from my super, I went into shock. I threw away the original key that I mailed him, and went upstairs to apologize to the whole family. I had no idea what was awaiting me.

Mr. Steemhed greeted me with clenched fists. "Uh huh, so you're the son of a bitch who owns this building. I should kick your ass for what you put my family through."

I didn't use profanity when responding. I didn't want to lose my false teeth. Remaining calm, I let him vent his anger, praying that he wouldn't sue me for medical bills paid in the hospital emergency room for thawing out five frostbitten rumps. Actually it was ten frost bitten rumps if you add both cheeks. I apologized over and over again until I felt he was calming down. I offered to reduce his rent $400 for the following month. But instead of thanking me, he said that he wouldn't accept less than $500. Why did I have to be so generous? Maybe he wouldn't have asked for a penny. I had to put my foot in it.

Gradually, for some unknown reason, our relationship improved. Since that first day, he has reined in his temper and become one of my best tenants.

CHAPTER EIGHT

THE GRASSY KNOLL

SORTING MY MAIL ONE summer day, I noticed a letter from the health department. It was a violation issued to me, dated one year earlier, for failing to remove tires, rims, hubcaps, construction material, rotten food, and other assorted garbage from one of my lots. in Cypress Hills Brooklyn. First of all, I have to congratulate the inspector for due diligence. People who fail to keep their property clean deserve to be fined the maximum that the law permits.

But there was one small problem. I didn't (and still don't) own a lot in or near Cypress Hills. The address written on the violation was for a building that I had sold eighteen months earlier in East New York and the date of the violation was dated two months before I sold the building. This means that when the inspector wrote the summons, I still owned the building. The block, lot number, and the imbecile inspector's name were all illegible. My name and address were legible. I understand that inspectors make mistakes, but this mistake caused me a myriad of problems. I wasn't sure what my first step should be, but knew that if I didn't move fast to prove my innocence, I could wind up paying a fortune in fines. I had already missed two scheduled court dates and the health department wasn't ready to schedule another one. My first step was going over to the building and asking the owner if he remembered seeing any kind of notice with my name on it.

"I did see something like you described," he said, "but it was not on the door, but in a pile of garbage that you never threw away. We didn't have time to haul it out to the sanitation guys for pickup, so we shoveled the pile into a box and pushed it into a far corner of the store so we didn't have to look at it. If you want, go take a look. Who knows? It may still be there."

I had nothing to lose. Not expecting to find anything, I swished the garbage pile around with a shovel. I saw something that looked like a violation. It was the same violation that I received in the mail, but printed on a different color of paper. I had found the original, but what the hell good did it do? I was still knee-deep in manure. My next move was driving to the health department for answers. But knowing the balloon heads working there, I didn't anticipate positive results.

Mrs. Dewnaut at the health department was very cooperative, bringing me the copy of the violation they had in their file. It was just as unclear as the other two. Everything was going against me and the clock was ticking, but I couldn't leave the place without answers. I politely asked Mrs. Dewnaut if there was some way to retrieve the name of the inspector who had issued the citation.

"I'll see what I can do," she said. Fifteen minutes later she returned. "I've got three inspectors who were in the area that day, but the problem is one of them went back to India, one is on vacation, and the other one was only in a few restaurants to see if the owners were complying with the health codes. I'm truly sorry, sir, but I can't help you."

"I'm sorry too, ma'am."

An idea came to me. The citation said that my alleged lot contained a grassy knoll. I could look at topographical maps in the building department to find lots in Cypress Hills with any elevated landforms. I looked at maps of the area, but the maps only showed structures and large undeveloped masses of land, nothing even close to the lot I was looking for. But I still felt I was in the right place. Perhaps I didn't know how to read the maps correctly. One of the clerks behind the desk surely would. I waited on line, ready to the do the jitterbug, confident I'd soon be yanked out of the manure. But just my luck, the clerks were idiots. Mr. Mapiless knew nothing about maps and Mr. Noluss, at the adjoining window, knew even less. I couldn't believe it. Two topographical scientists working in the Queens map section, and neither one was able to read a map. I was back to square one, with the fine going up by the day. There was only one thing left to do. I had no choice but drive up and down every block in the entire area until I found the right lot. The clock was ticking. If I didn't come up with a solution fast, there was no telling how much the fine would be. Not only that, but I'd be labeled as another slumlord evading the law. Just then something dawned on me. Maybe, just maybe, the inspector had written the correct street on the summons but the wrong numbers. But on second thought, how could it be? He was only responsible for the six-block radius surrounding my building. Suddenly, Sherlock Holmes whispered in my ear from the rear that maybe the inspector was heading to my building and, on the way, saw the lot. Though it was outside his territory, he felt it was his duty to issue a summons, writing on it my address by mistake. Because he couldn't find the owner or place to post the summons, he called his office, asking someone to tell him the name of the owner matching the wrong address on the summons. My building is on a street twenty-four blocks long. I had only checked the street seven blocks in each direction. For the hell of it, I did what Sherlock suggested, even though Watson was unavailable for confirmation. Starting from my building I drove west, constantly looking to the right and to the left, praying to get lucky. As I approached the end of the block on the right side, I saw a small lot filled with assorted garbage matching the inspector's description, except I didn't see any tires or tire rims. This was not the lot. But I wasn't dead yet. Perhaps the lot I wanted was on the east end of the block. So I immediately reversed direction and drove east. Just as I crossed the intersection of the 23rd block I spotted some high grass. Could this finally be it? I walked between a couple small shacks and, sure enough, there was a huge lot with three or four tires and some tire rims. This had to be it. I took pictures of the lot from every conceivable angle. I gathered pictures of my building where the violation was posted on the door for comparison to the lot that didn't belong to me, and my warning letter, and drove to the building department to match the block and lot number to the right owner. Instead of mailing my package of proof, I drove to the health department and I physically handed the package to the clerk at the counter and demanded a receipt"

We don't give receipts," he said. I couldn't believe what I heard. It wasn't enough that I was innocent of this horrendous infraction, running every which way to prove it. But now I had to listen to this stupid jerk tell me that he would not give me a receipt. "What if someone lost or misplaced my bundle of evidence? I asked. "The building department is notorious for that. "We're not the building department. This is the health department," he said.

"How comforting." I left praying that some balloon head clerk wouldn't screw up. Sure enough, one of them did. That did it! I sent another set of copies. But this time, I didn't want another trap door episode, so I sent the package certified mail return receipt requested, not just certified mail. Glory Glory hallelujah they received the package and soon afterwards wrote me a letter of apology. They removed the violation from my records informing me that a court appearance and certificate of correction were not necessary. I kept the letter of apology nearby in case I ran out of toilet paper. Eventually the health department, at my request, wrote another letter to me that explained in detail what had transpired from beginning to end.

CHAPTER NINE

ECB STORY#1

MY RELATIONSHIP WITH THE ECB has been stormy from day one. I know that they are a necessary part of city governance, but they have heaped problems and frustrations on me, which include lack of reasons for issuing a violation, kangaroo court decisions, inspectors writing the name of the building owner on the summons instead of the tenant when, according to the lease, the tenant is responsible. The ECB does not differentiate between the two. I could go on and on, but it would require several more pages. The following stories illustrate my frustration.

Jimmy Squatnick, a tenant of mine, told me that he had seen an ECB inspector walking in front of my building on Smith Street. This was the building I bought from Comenser in 1979. The building measures fifty-four feet from the building surface to the curb. There are parking meters on the entire block. The inspector didn't find any garbage on the side walk so he headed straight to the street, looking for garbage between the tires and curb of two cars parked there. He must have found something because Squatnick saw him write two tickets. Copies of the tickets were mailed to me. The tickets read, "I observed litter between the tires and curb of two cars parked in front of 112-08 and 112-06 Smith street. There was room for the broom." The litter was within the 18" space off the curb that is the landlord's responsibility to clean. Because of those tickets I had to wait more than three hours in Kangaroo court to see an administrative pseudo-judge who sits behind a desk, determining how much he can screw the person sitting across from him.

All pseudo-judges have a book in their desk drawer listing the minimum and maximum fine they can impose. You can contest the decision but the appeal board won't even read your appeal until you pay the fine. You need an ironclad case to even have a chance of winning an appeal. Maybe it's because the pseudo-judges and appeal board were in the same fraternity. My lucky draw was a pseudo-judge with Spock-like ears and a nose large enough to fit a roll of nickels in each nostril. Yes, this is irrelevant, but how could I resist mentioning it if I had felt compelled to make eye contact?

"You are charged with failure to remove garbage that the inspector saw between the tires and curb of two separate cars parked directly in front of 112-06 Smith Street and 112-08 Smith Street. The inspector states in the summons that there was room for a broom. How do you plead?"

"Guilty, ahem . . . with an explanation, your honor."

But my explanation wouldn't matter. The ECB is smart. When you plead not guilty, you have to come back a second time to face the inspector. They know damn well many of the accused can't afford to waste another day in court. It's easier to just pay the fine, but if a defendant insists on taking things further, whom do you think the judge will believe, the cited party or the inspector?

But I kept going. "I would like to say a few things, your honor."

"Go ahead, Mr. Carlos but it better be relevant."

"This is a very busy commercial street, your honor. No one is allowed to park between eight a.m. and eight-thirty a.m. on the entire block so the city sanitation department has the necessary space to sweep away all the debris. Doesn't that indicate, your honor that the city knows it's practically impossible for a landlord to keep up with all the garbage piling up? Does the ECB honestly expect me to order my super to get down on his knees and reach under the car with his hands or broom to remove garbage? And not only that, your honor, he could lose his hand if he didn't notice the driver entering his car and suddenly pulling out. The same thing applies to a driver suddenly zooming into the spot. I can't, for the life of me, your honor, understand this 'room for the broom law.' On all the busy streets in commercial areas, a driver is worried about passing cars knocking out his side mirror, so they park as close to the curb as possible. How can anybody have enough room between the tires and curb to squeeze in a broom? Even if you did manage to ram it in there, how could you possibly move the broom in any of the four directions?"

"Let me explain the law to you, sir," the pseudo-judge said. "It's the landlord's responsibility to keep his property clean. It doesn't matter if your building is one hundred feet from the curb or the tires are one inch off the curb. This is your building and you are the one responsible for maintaining it. If one broom doesn't work, buy another one. This hearing is over. You will receive my decision in the mail."

Two weeks later, I learned my fate. The lousy, blood-sucking ECB made me pay them $200, $100 for each address. This is just one example of how the ECB keeps the money rolling in, completely disregarding ethics and fairness.

CHAPTER TEN

ECB STORY#2

ON TWO DIFFERENT DATES in the summer of 1995, two street vendors parked their hot dog stands at the curbside fifty feet away from the front of of my building at 112-06 Smith st.. The police shut both of them down shortly after they started doing business. I didn't know about it until a year and a half later when I was trying to refinance the building.

My credit was excellent, my mortgage payments were on time, and the building was free of violations. The property was worth a lot more than the money I wanted to borrow, so I was positive the bank would cooperate. I was so sure that I signed an affidavit that if we didn't close within sixty days, the bank could swallow my 10-percent down payment. At the closing, everything was going smoothly but just as the bank rep was about to hand me the check, the title company representative shouted out to stop the proceedings.

"I'm sorry, people, we can't close," she yelled.

"What?" I shouted. "What the hell does that mean?"

"It means, sir, that the bank will not give you the money until two ECB violations are removed from the record."

I refused to let her off the hook. "Correct me if I am wrong, madam, but isn't it the title company's job to learn if there are any violations prior to the closing?"

"Yes," she said. "You're right, but these violations were issued directly to two different hot dog vendors parked on your sidewalk eighteen months ago. The unpaid tickets were issued to the vendors, not to you, so even though your name doesn't appear anywhere; a lien was placed on your property. Because the violation is relatively new, the lien only appeared on the public record ten days ago. One of our people just now found out about it. To compound matters, the address in question was a corner building in the name of a corporation, with the legally recorded address on Pauper Street. The vendor's carts were parked on Smith Street, the only street appearing on the violation."

I sympathized with the title company, but this was a real pain. I asked the bank rep how much time I had to settle this thing so the bank wouldn't change their mind about lending me money?

"I don't know, sir," he said. "But if you want to dispose of the matter immediately, you have to pay $2,500 to the ECB for each violation and get a receipt from their office proving to us that you have paid them. "Also, we have to check their website to see that the violation has been removed from record. I thanked everyone for the good news and told them that I'd take care of the problem.

"That's fine, sir, but keep in mind, if you take too long we may have to raise the interest rate on your loan a half a percent."

That sounds like chicken feed, but with the amount of money we're looking at, it was significant. "I understand Sir" I said. "I'll move on it as fast as I can."

If I didn't dispose of this mess within forty-five days, I'd lose my 10 percent down payment. That damn well wasn't going to happen to me. I sped down to the ECB office, my favorite hellhole, and headed straight to the information desk. I showed Miss Karing, the attractive young lady at the desk, copies of the violations, politely asking her permission to see a judge.

"I doubt that you can," she said. "You are in default. In order to see him, you must write a letter to the ECB, requesting the case be reopened. But I'm not sure they'll agree. You waited too long."

I was getting nowhere. I begged her to see the judge. I guess it helped because she gave me a smile and went back to the hearing section to try circumventing normal procedure. Ten minutes later, Miss Karing returned with the head clerk. I knew from her expression that I was a dead duck.

"I'm very sorry, sir, "she said. The judge will not see you. Your name is not on the summons. He said the only thing you can do is get both vendors to write a letter to the ECB requesting the case be reopened, and instruct them to have their signatures notarized. The same procedure applies if they want you to act on their behalf."

I couldn't believe my ears. That was the last straw. Two hot dog vendors go free without paying a dime, and I had no time to avoid paying their fines. I asked Miss Karing what the total would be if I paid right then. I still wish that I hadn't. The two hot dog vendors owed the city, between them, over $5,000, exactly what the bank rep told me. This included interest and late fees. I stood on line with twenty more suckers and paid the $5,000 fine, and then I stood on another line for at least thirty minutes, chewing my fingernails and clawing my sweaty palms, until I finally got the letter of satisfaction that the bank demanded. Only the lord above knew how angry I was. I was lucky the bank representative was a decent guy, or I would have paid a considerably higher interest rate on the loan, or even lost the deal altogether.

CHAPTER ELEVEN

THE KEMPT SISTERS

MALLORY AND DOLORES KEMPT were two residential tenants that I inherited as an unfortunate consequence of a mid-nineties building purchase. Sadly, neither of these jewels found it necessary to hang their clothes, wash dishes more than once a week, or wash laundry more than twice a year. I believe the best two-word description of their apartment is "pig sty." There were open cans of food all over the apartment, spoiled meat on the kitchen counter drawing flies, and last, but definitely not least, cardboard boxes piled up to the ceiling in every room except the bathroom. The bathroom was nearly inaccessible.

They were always reluctant to let me into the apartment. One reason was their unfounded fear that if I bought them a stove or fridge, I'd be entitled to the benefits of the J-51 Capital Improvement program, entitling me to raise their rent. Their stove was missing three knobs, forcing them to use pliers to adjust the flame, and their refrigerator was barely working. Several floor tiles needed replacing. The only thing they let me do was paint. If they refused to let me in the apartment to do repair work, I'd need a judge to order them to comply.

Jack Presto, my lawyer, had a reputation for getting results fast. I was hoping he might help me kill two birds with one stone. First, I wanted a judge to order the sisters to clean their apartment and give me a key to their front door to be used only in the event of emergency. Second, I wanted permission to renovate or replace anything I deemed necessary. After three court sessions of haggling between my lawyer and theirs, we reached an agreement. The judge ordered the Sisters to let my people into the apartment to do what we had to do.

Now that I was partially victorious, I started to feel confident that the two darlings would be more cooperative. Surprisingly, none of the other tenants in the building complained to the health department or any other city agency about the rancid odor permeating the hallways. There was no doubt in my mind that the apartment should have been labeled a health hazard. I instructed my lawyer to push for an order that would force the sisters to clean their apartment.

Jack Presto addressed Judge Partway. "Your honor, the Kempt sisters apartment is a deplorable mess. It's definitely a health hazard. I respectfully request your honor to demand that the Slob sisters clean up their apartment as soon as possible."

"Unless there are numerous complaints, my hands are tied," the Judge said.

Lightning Jack responded, "I can understand that, your honor, but what about all those boxes my client saw piled up to the ceiling?"

"Let me remind you, Mr. Presto, if the sisters are eating in the apartment, sleeping in the apartment and using the bathroom facilities, I don't care how many boxes they have in there, or how many other things are scattered over the floor, they have the right to reside in their apartment free of disturbance."

"We will obviously abide by your decision, your honor. But my client told me that there was no way to enter the bathroom without swinging from the ceiling like an orangutan. Doesn't this represent a dangerous condition, your honor?"

"Listen young man, maybe they play orangutan games from time to time. How do I know?" The judge wasn't laughing. "Anyhow, it's none of your business. Oh, one other thing: Tell your client that it would be a waste of time to call the health department. He will probably get an answer similar to mine." The judge remained stoic. "By the way, just out of curiosity, did you actually see them jumping or climbing? If not, I suggest you refrain from speculation."

Totally frustrated, I returned home, mumbling profanity all the way to the front door. These two Slob sisters had me by the tennis balls. But I had an idea. If I called the health department, pretending that I was a tenant, and complained that I saw rats running up and down the hallway, squeezing their way under a door, they'd be there in a flash. The rat story was a lie, but once the health department inspector was inside the apartment and saw the atrocious conditions, there's no way he'd fail to issue the Slob sisters a summons.

My tactic worked at first. Two inspectors came and inspected the entire apartment, but didn't see any mice or rat feces. They filed their report and left without saying a word. Two weeks later, I received a summons in the mail, ordering me to pay the NYC department of health $2,000 for ignoring serious health hazard conditions. I knew appealing would be a waste of time. To rub it in, the Slob sisters complained that their front door was broken. Upon examination, I saw that it was impossible to repair. I was obligated to either fix the door or buy a new one. By the way, did I mention that this was their third door? These two darlings cost me a bundle. Between lawyers, fines, court appearances, new appliances, mailbox keys, mailbox repairs and doors, I paid at least $15,000. It took me three years to recover. The Slob sisters are still my tenants.

CHAPTER TWELVE

BEDBUGS

BEDBUGS ARE ANOTHER SOURCE of rear-end discomfort. Every month or two, a tenant of mine calls the health department complaining about bedbugs. When I hear the word "bedbug," it's like waving a red flag in front of my face. I tell every complainer very succinctly that I do not supply bedbugs. They're not included in the lease. If a tenant brings them in, let him or her evict them at their own expense. Bedbugs are usually found in used mattresses, box springs and the clothing on your back, but you can't force the tenant to buy new mattresses or wash his clothes thoroughly the second he enters the apartment.

What really drives me nuts is when the tenant calls the health department before letting me know. The minute the health department is notified, the landlord is put on notice to eliminate the bedbugs ASAP or face a fine. Once the word leaks out in the building, another tenant may complain, just to get a new mattress. It costs me $1,600 to spray two apartments, and there's no guarantee the spray will be effective. I could bitch to the health department, but do you actually think someone there is going to listen? Getting rid of bedbugs permanently is impossible. To this day, no one has found a solution.

CHAPTER THIRTEEN

THE COMMERCIAL BONANZA

THIS COMMERCIALLY ZONED RESIDENTIAL colonial house in Queens, with thirty five hundred square feet of land, turned to be the most profitable purchase of my real estate career. The owners who sold us the house were an elderly doctor and his ailing wife. The price was so cheap that I didn't even need a mortgage. This was around the same time that I purchased my first building from Comenser. As soon as the couple vacated, I found a tenant to occupy the entire house.

PART I: JUDY CONEMALL

MY TENANT, JUDY CONEMALL, was a want to be entrepreneur, looking to make a fortune ASAP. She worked with a dishonest appraiser who overvalued properties, a dishonest bank insider who falsified credit ratings, and carefully chosen dishonest sellers, all working in concert with her to bilk the bank. For example, Judy would buy a property that was appraised as more valuable than it really was. The bank insider would give her a mortgage based on the phony appraisal. The seller would kick back to the appraiser and the appraiser would kick back to the bank insider. The bank insider made sure to delete from the system any bad credit reports so involved applicants would be eligible for a loan. Judy would rent then out the property for as long as possible, not paying the bank a penny. When the property was near foreclosure, the foreclosure process takes about a year, Judy would kick out the tenant or tenants, pocket all the rent money, buy another property, and together with her fellow criminals, continue working the same scam. I had no idea about any of this when she was a tenant, only finding out one or two years later when I saw her face in the newspaper. This was around the time several savings-and-loan banks went under, possibly due to similar scams.

During her tenancy with my permission, she added an extension of seven retail stores to the property. I told her it was okay as long as she agreed to do everything in accordance with the building department codes and zoning regulations. I didn't care if she pocketed all the money from the sublets, as long as she paid me my rent. She convinced me that she'd do everything legally. Gullible Mr. Carlos believed her. The extension was built in two months. Three weeks later, she had rented out all seven stores.

Eight months later, while collecting the rent, I saw, to my utter surprise that her office was completely empty. I couldn't figure it out. She had paid me like clockwork on the first of every month. Just in case she returned, I waited another week before placing an ad in the paper for a new tenant. The ad proved worthless. This was a house, but classified as commercial, not residential. Few people are willing to run a retail business from a house. But all was not lost. I just inherited seven tenants without lifting a finger. How lucky can you get? I was making so much money from them that I didn't need a new tenant to replace Judy Conemall. I milked the stores for six or seven months until, finally, the cow ran out of milk. While I was talking to one of the storeowners, an inspector from the building department, a Mr. Rayzit, dropped in.

"Are you the owner?" he asked.

"Yes sir," I answered. "What can I do for you?"

"Are you aware, sir, that all these stores are illegal?"

"No, I didn't know," I said.

"Well, I hate to say it, but you better knock them all down. And it better be done yesterday."

"Why?" I asked. "If there are violations, can't I correct them to avoid this?"

"There are way too many violations to even bother explaining," he said.

I saw it was useless to argue with him. I hired an architect to prepare a blueprint for a completely new commercial structure, consisting of eight legal retail spaces divided between the lower level, first floor, and second floor. After the architect's plans were approved, I hired a demolition team to raze the house and a construction contractor to set the project in motion. As soon as the new building was erected and passed inspection, I was able to obtain a CO (certificate of occupancy) in less than four months.

PART II: THE VICTIMS

Store space #1 was rented to a small wholesale hardware distributor named John Scruedover. Store space #2 was rented to a travel agent named Mrs. Goesome. Store space #3, I rented to a computer repairman named Mr. Fixt. Store space #4, I rented to a shoemaker named Mr. Soleless. Store space #5, I rented to a pharmacist named Mr. Treeter. Store #6, I rented to a photographer named Mr. Scenick, and last, I rented store #7 to a Physical Therapist named Dr. Twistem. The income generated from this new building far exceeded my expectations, but you will soon see that all was not peaches and cream.

One month before the tenants moved in, I arranged to have an electric meter and a gas meter installed for each one. Each tenant was responsible for his or her own usage. First, I called the gas company. The dispatcher, Mrs. Asistor, who later changed her name to Stupehdow, told me that she'd send a person the following week, sometime between eight a.m. and seven p.m. I told her this was wonderful but asked if she could narrow down the time slot.

"I have no control over these things," she said. "The installers set their own timetable."

I tried to speak to a supervisor but got nowhere. Seeing I had no choice, I sent Limpy, my best loiterer, to hang around the building for as long as it took. At five p.m., I had the pleasure of meeting the installer. His name was Tony Maymix. I was lucky Limpy only had to wait on the sidewalk eight hours and did not have to spend the night. I'm also grateful that Limpy's loitering only cost me $80. I stood there watching Mr. Maymix until he finished installing the meter. Before too long, he picked up his tool kit, telling me he was going to a nearby diner for something to eat. I told him that he could leave his stuff in the boiler room until he returned.

"What for?" he asked. "I'm not coming back. My orders were to install one meter, and nothing more."

"Install one meter? Who the hell told you that?" I shouted. "My guy had to stand on the sidewalk for eight miserable hours, waiting for someone to install one lousy meter?" Before finishing my sentence, he was gone.

I was so fucking mad that I could have literally strangled someone. To avoid a repeat with the next meter installation, I called the gas company and asked to speak to a supervisor. The woman answering the phone told me to wait on the line until she found one. I wasn't lucky enough to have a speakerphone so I had to hold the lousy phone to my ear for twenty minutes until some moron finally picked up. Who do you think the moron was? It was the same woman that I had spoken to twenty minutes ago. Adding fuel to the fire, she asked me how she could provide me with outstanding service. Hearing this always sends chills throughout my entire body. I will never understand why any employer with a theoretically normal brain would make their employee ask such a stupid question.

I tried my best to be nice. "What is your name, sweetie?" I asked.

"Miss Doozy," she said.

"That's a lovely name," I said. "Maybe you could handle my problem instead of transferring me to a supervisor."

"I'll do my best," she said. I explained to her my predicament and frustration.

"I can't help you with that, sir. I'll have to transfer you to a supervisor. But before I do, could you please tell me if I provided you with outstanding service today?"

That did it. My nervous system couldn't take it any more. I slammed down the phone and drove straight to the gas company to speak face to face with a supervisor. Mr. Dimwitter, the supervisor, lived up to his name, and didn't offer any assistance. I saw that I was beating a dead horse, so I returned home sulking like a little boy that just lost his rubber ball to a nerd half his size. The following week, three more meters were installed, each on a separate day. I couldn't understand why I had to pay for it. The gas company had told me the installation would be free of charge.

I had also paid Limpy $270 for the thirty-two hours he had stood on the sidewalk awaiting four different installers. I had to find a way to circumvent this stupidity. I told Limpy to go home and let me take his place, waiting for the next installer. My plan was to grease the installer, praying he wouldn't report me and that he'd be the the last gas company installer I'd have to see for the rest of my life The installer finally showed up, took my $100 and inserted the remaining three meters. He told me not to worry because his girlfriend worked in customer service for the gas company, and would doctor the computer records to make it look like each meter was installed on a different day. I thought that the worst was over. The truth is the worst was just beginning. One or more of the installers incorrectly wired some meters, connecting them to the wrong store, meaning that some storeowners were going to pay for another storeowner's bills. No one, including me, was aware of this until one year later, in April, when the tenants received their bills for the previous two months' usage. The winter before had been so mild most of the tenants kept their thermostats off or at a low setting.

The fun started when I received a phone call from my tenant in #1, Mr. Scruedover, complaining about his gas bill. He told me that it was way too high for a store of only five hundred square feet, and the gas company was charging him at least double. When he showed me that the bill was based on an actual reading, I was inclined to agree with him. Mr. Scruedover could hardly speak English, so I called the gas company on his behalf, asking them to reread the meter. As I was already on the scene, I went to each of the other stores to see if they were getting heat. The owners of the #2 and #3 stores said everything was fine.

Mr. Soleless in store #4 reported good news. "Yeah, Mr. Carlos, but I can't believe that my gas bill was so cheap. I got two thousand square feet here. And it says on the bill it was an actual reading. I simply can't believe it, but what do I care? I wasn't going to look a gift horse in the mouth."

We both started laughing. But suddenly an unhappy realization dawned on me. Scruedover in store #1 was complaining about paying too much for such a small space. Mr. Soleless is laughing about getting a ridiculously low bill for his large space. Had the meter reader fucked up twice? I don't believe in coincidences. Something was definitely rotten in Denmark. I proceeded to store #5. Mr. Treeter, like Scruedover in store #1, was also getting screwed. Store #6, Mr. Scenick the photographer, said everything was fine. Thank the lord for small favors. Dr. Twistem in the #7 store was shrieking like a soprano who just won the lottery.

"I just looked at my gas bill," he said. "I can't believe it. My bill is practically nothing, but I sure won't complain."

"That's great," I said.

While driving home, I realized that the meters must have been crossed. I wasn't sure what I could do to solve the problem. At the time, I only knew what *not* to do. For one, I would not call the gas company to report it. That would be a waste of time.

They would definitely tell me that they had put the right tag number on each meter and did not get involved in commercial disputes. My only recourse was to relabel the meters. I would then inform all the tenants of what had happened and sit down with the over—and undercharged storeowners to settle on a mutually agreeable reimbursement. Don't ask me how much I paid them to shut up. Oh, wait a minute, I almost forgot: Dr. Twistem in store #7 also screwed somebody, but as none of the remaining store owners opened their mouths, I also kept mine shut, hoping this one sleeping dog would stay asleep. Finally, don't ask how long it took the ass company—excuse me, Gas Company—to update their computers.

CHAPTER FOURTEEN

THE MEDICAL OFFICE

ONE BRIGHT SUNNY DAY, a stretch limo pulled up to my building at 112-08 Smith Street and out stepped three distinguished elderly gentleman. One of them asked if my basement space was still available. To find a commercial tenant for a basement is not easy, so I didn't hesitate to say yes. Vladimir, who assumed the role of spokesman for the three, said that they needed about three thousand square feet to set up a third Bilkum Inc. medical facility. After the three men inspected the basement, they told me that it was exactly what they were looking for and were ready to sign a lease with me. I was so happy that I was ready to dance a jig without music. They never questioned the amount of the rent. We entered into a five-year lease with the tenant's option to renew. I could prevent them from renewing only if I had reasonable grounds.

Two months later, after extensive renovation, their business was ready to open. The facility provided treatment for everything from A to Z, except for gynecology. I didn't want to step on the toes of the gynecologist already open on the second floor. My new tenants were busier than bees from day one. People were coming and going from morning to night. The rent checks were in my hand no later than the third day of each month. I couldn't stop thanking the good lord for giving me such wonderful tenants. Also, Ivan, the manager of the facility, provided me with two massages a month at a discount rate. But then, like my father used to say, all good things must come to an end. My father was no dummy. Two and a half years into their lease, Ivan, who was not only my tenant, but also became a good friend, notified me that there was a distinct possibility they would be moving their operation to Kansas. This was terrible news. His wife and my wife had also formed a warm relationship. My wife had them over for dinner at least four times. To hear him say he'd be gone in a matter of two months was simply too much to bear. Six months later, Ivan informed me that his boss was closing down my location and transferring it to the Bronx.

"What happened to Kansas?" I asked. "You told me you were moving to Kansas."

"That's right," he said. "But there was a last minute shuffle at the top. But look at the bright side, Carlos, I'm still going to be the director, but in the Bronx, not here. We have each other's phone numbers and I'm only a half-hour away."

Finally, moving day arrived. I lost both a good tenant and good friend at the same time, and was stuck with three thousand square feet of empty commercial space. I didn't need to be told that this space would be vacant for a long time. I kept in touch with Ivan for a few months until he disconnected his phone. After that, the only time I heard from him was when he called me from an unknown number, asking if any of his mail was sent to me by mistake?

About two years later, I received a registered letter from a government agency inviting me to visit their office on the following Friday to answer some questions. The letter was vague, so I called the number at the top of the letterhead for an explanation. The man answering the phone asked if I had rented space to a medical facility called Bilkum, Inc.

"Yes, sir. Is there a problem?" I asked.

Ignoring my question, he continued. "Did you have a lease with them? If so, bring it with you on Friday. Also bring all the information they supplied you prior to signing the lease."

I asked to know what was going on.

"You'll know everything when you get here," he said.

I had bad vibes. Something was wrong. What did I do? I'm only a landlord. Let these government people ask Ivan and other members of the Bilkum hierarchy all the questions they want. I was scared that they'd nail me for something I had nothing to do with, so instead of waiting for Friday's question and answer session, I offered to send the agency all the information I had by Federal Express, which included the lease, photos, ID, bank statements, references, tax returns, copies of rent checks, and history of their operation. It did the trick. I never heard from them again.

CHAPTER FIFTEEN

MR. RATINVYTE

GETTING RID OF RATS is one of the most difficult tasks a landlord confronts. I once had a tenant threaten to punch me in the nose if I didn't eliminate rats from his rental fast enough. Rats can squeeze through the smallest cracks. As soon as a rat finds accommodations suitable, he'll return to the nearby construction lot where he resides and bring back his immediate family. Once the guest rooms are ready, friends and relatives will follow. It won't be a problem finding the place. They simply follow the feces trail.

Mr. Ratinvyte, a tenant in one of my two-bedroom apartments, was named appropriately. I don't mean to imply he was a rat. He simply had a unique ability to draw rodents. Before renting to him, I had asked the usual questions. For example, did your last landlord throw you out, or did you leave voluntarily? This was what I considered comprehensive questioning. I made it clear to him I wouldn't allow more than five people to live in the apartment. Obviously, it wasn't important to ask if he planned to comply. I inspected the apartment before Ratinvyte moved in, making sure all interior doorknobs, other than the bedrooms, were keyless. If they had key slots, it was a sure sign that the tenant was illegally subletting. Sure enough, a few days after Mr. Ratinvyte, moved in, without my knowledge, he changed three doorknobs from keyless to key slot and sublet to lord only knows how many people. A week later, I started hearing rumors from one of the other tenants in my building that way too many people were living in the apartment, and that tons of garbage was piling up on the grass next to the Dumpster. When the rats started coming, the fun began. Mr. Ratinvyte called me at home, warning me that if I didn't do something about the rats fast, he'd call the health department. His tone of voice hardly sounded like the same man that I had met and leased to just weeks before.

"What rats?" I asked. "When did you see rats?"

"I called you two days ago, leaving a message, but you never called back," he said.

This was a lie. I was reluctant to call the health department because I was sure they'd stick me with a fine. There was only one thing left to do: get rid of the rats myself. I still didn't know that Ratinvyte had changed the doorknobs and squeezed extra people into the apartment. He was starting to get irritable and hot under the collar. I kept quiet and let him ramble on. Before we ended our chat, he told me that he wanted to see me, "face to face."

To be perfectly honest, I was scared shitless. I was shaking in my boots all the way to his apartment. The guy weighed about two hundred and fifty pounds and stood about six feet four inches tall. I thought about bringing a baseball bat with me for protection but changed my mind. What would I do if he used it on me?

I knocked on his door, expecting him to be angry. I wasn't disappointed.

"Listen, you prick, he said, if you don't get rid of these rats, I'm going to make you a new face. "Are we communicating?" he asked. I mustered all my strength and promised him that I'd get the job done as fast as humanly possible.

"I don't want promises; I want results," he said.

Too bad I still didn't know how many people were living in the apartment. At least then I would have had leverage. On my way out, he gave me a nasty look. It was the kind of look that showed he meant business.

I called an exterminating company and explained my predicament to the girl who answered the phone. She told me that she had just the right person for me.

"What do you mean?" I asked.

"The guy I'm talking about is a licensed professional hit man with a reputation for killing anything walking on four or more legs, but I warn you, he doesn't come cheap."

"How much is not cheap?"

"Five hundred bucks for starters," she said.

Tiny Finito, the hit man in question, said that he would place four small poison-treated wood blocks in the kitchen area, and emphasized that nobody should set foot in the apartment for two days while he worked. I sensed that he enjoyed killing things. The way he explained how the rat would nibble away at the block and die a few hours later made him chuckle. He was only five feet three inches tall, hardly the size expected of a professional hit man. Maybe his tiny stature worked to his advantage, allowing him to make close eye contact with the rats, causing them to drop dead on the spot. Who knows. Maybe I could save some money on the blocks?

I explained the plan to Ratinvyte, making sure that he had Finito's telephone number and vice versa.

A few days later, Ratinvyte started calling me. I ignored him for a couple days, but couldn't avoid the inevitable. I finally called him, asking if he had noticed that any of the blocks had been nibbled. "I wasn't there Mr. Landlord. As far as I know, the rats didn't nibble, chew, swallow, or, even sniff the motherfucking blocks. You get your ass up here now and take all this crap out of here. I'm not going to tell you again."

Because I valued my life, I sent someone else to do what Ratinvyte asked.

I was back to square one. There were rats in the backyard, rats in the apartment, and one big rat named Ratinvyte threatening to change my face. Suddenly, I had a flash of insight. Maybe my friend Jeremy the diamond dealer could spare Tiger for a few days.

CHAPTER SIXTEEN

ROOSEVELT AND TIGER

TIGER WAS AN OVER sized cat, more like a small jaguar. I was positive that he could tear to shreds any rat. There was no doubt in my mind that Tiger could get me out of this mess. Jeremy agreed to lend me the cat. Wonderful, but how the hell could I handle such a big animal all by myself? Jeremy said he could also lend me "the Monster Man," Roosevelt Monsterman, his six-foot-eight-inch-tall, 260-pound bodyguard.

Roosevelt proved to be a lifesaver. He and I hit it off from day one. I convinced him to accompany me the next time I visited Ratinvyte. If Ratinvyte wasn't afraid of me, he surely would be afraid of Roosevelt. My new bodyguard put a leash around Tiger's neck and led him to the backseat of my car. This was no easy job. Once Tiger was comfortably seated, Roosevelt opened the back window to give the kitty some air. When we had to stop for a red light, an elderly lady driving a Cadillac pulled up alongside us. The second that she saw Tiger, she freaked out and floored the accelerator, zooming through a red light. Luckily, she didn't kill anyone, but she did drive across someones lawn, destroying a flowerbed and smashing a couple of flowerpots. As we drove away, I told Roosevelt to tell the cat to keep its head down.

We reached Ratinvyte's building. Roosevelt opened the back door of the car, holding the cat's leash with all his might to prevent Tiger from bolting.

Now I could confront Ratinvyte with confidence instead of trepidation. I rang his bell and he yanked open the door.

Completely ignoring Roosevelt, he asked "What's that fucking monster doing here? It belongs in the fucking jungle, not around people."

Roosevelt remained quiet, but kept his eyes on Ratinvyte. With all my strength, similar to my first meeting with Mr. Longalux in Cypress Hills, I stretched my neck to its fullest extent, trying to make eye contact with Ratinvyte. "This here cat is moving in," I said. "You have two choices. One: stay here. Two: move out."

Ratinvyte exploded like Mt. Vesuvius. "No rotten, stinking jungle cat is coming into this apartment," he said. "So you can take your pussy cat, along with your pussy friend, and get the fuck out of my sight before I beat the crap out of both of you."

Roosevelt could no longer remain silent. He grabbed Ratinvyte by his collar, squeezing it around his neck so tight that it closed off his windpipe. "Listen, you piece of shit, you do what Mr. Carlos tells you, or I'll put you in the hospital permanently. You understand."

Suddenly, Mr. Ratinvyte turned from a lion to a whimpering mouse. Roosevelt had already earned his money. Now I was totally in charge. I told him to wait for me a minute. Without Ratinvyte's permission, I did what I had wanted to do for some time: enter every room in the apartment to check for damage. I wasn't thinking, at that moment, about the possibility of too many people living there.

Ratinvyte followed me into the back rooms, but Roosevelt stopped him.

I saw that both bedrooms had knobs with key slots. That was okay, but as I walked farther into the apartment, I saw that all the remaining doors also had knobs with key slots. It didn't take a Rhodes scholar to figure it out. There were too many people living in the apartment. The only thing I didn't know was how many. I didn't have to fear Ratinvyte any longer.

"You are a liar, mister," I said. "You told me that there were only four people in your apartment. You have twenty-four hours to throw out all the people not belonging here. If you don't, I'll let Roosevelt do it for you." Ratinvyte cringed in fear.

The next day, Ratinvyte changed all the doorknobs except for the bedrooms. I made sure that Tiger had enough cat food to last him a week. I sure as hell didn't want to read on page one of the newspaper that a starving jungle animal resembling a cat had inhaled one of my tenants. The next day, the apartment was empty. I guessed between Roosevelt and the cat, everyone was too scared to remain. I couldn't help grinning from ear to ear.

The following day, Tiger disappeared. We looked in all the rooms, including closets, with no luck. Suddenly, I heard Roosevelt shouting from one of the bedrooms like he had been stuck in the rear end with a pitchfork.

"What happened, man?" I asked.

"Two motherfucking rats just ran between my legs," he shouted. "Where the hell is that damn cat?"

I noticed that one of the windows in the other bedroom was wide open. I went to close it so rain wouldn't get in, and I spotted our elusive friend Tiger running around in the backyard, chasing birds from one end of the lot to the other. I couldn't believe it, calling Roosevelt to come and watch the show. Both of us were dumbfounded, breaking into spontaneous laughter. My idea had turned out to be a big bust, but all was not lost. I was still pretty sure that Ratinvyte was too scared to take me to court, because I could either send Roosevelt after him or bring Tiger back to gobble him up for a snack. Seeing as Tiger was of no use, I asked Roosevelt to take the pitiful excuse for a cat back to Jeremy.

That evening, while relaying the rat story to my thirteen-year-old son, he interrupted me. "Cats are only good for killing mice," he said. "Big or small, they're all scared of rats. It's too bad you didn't know that ahead of time, but I have an idea for you."

Up to then, everything I'd tried to get rid of the rats had failed, so what could I lose by listening?

"Okay, so first, position six rat traps in a circle on the living room carpet and place tiny portions of raw meat on all of the six traps. After that, put another trap in the middle of the circle. On that one, put a huge amount of raw meat. Rats are smart. They'll probably sense danger from the outer traps but the extra-large portion of raw meat on the seventh trap will be too tempting to resist. If a rat doesn't get his paw stuck in one of the six outer traps, he should, with so little room to maneuver, get stuck jumping in or out of the inner circle."

I did exactly what my son told me to do. Three days later, I went to check on the apartment. I was entering the living room when I heard some kind of hissing or rubbing sound. It was a rat dragging itself across the carpet with his rear foot caught in one of the traps The rat had a mean, scary look in his eyes, definitely not the look of a domesticated pet. I wasn't ready to stand on ceremony. Animal League or no Animal League, Humane Society or no Humane Society, it was the rat or me, simple as that. I went to my car and brought back a snow shovel. The rat was already in one of the bedrooms. Before it had a chance to go under the bed, I smashed the ugly mother with the shovel two or three times as hard as I could. The pain from the bludgeoning caused the wounded rat to shriek at an ultra-high pitch, a warning sign to the other gnarling terrorists to take off immediately and find new surroundings. Ratinvyte never came back. Roosevelt's services cost me plenty, but it was worth every penny.

I was pretty sure that I was finally free of Ratinvyte, rats, and all the others living in the apartment. If the building department or health department had been tipped off, I would have paid them a lot more money for a fine than the money I had paid Roosevelt. The next tenant living in the apartment was a sweetheart, but instead of merely saying, "No story there," I'm compelled to make an exception with the following tale.

CHAPTER SEVENTEEN

THE LOST REFRIGERATOR

A LANDLORD IS REQUIRED to accommodate a tenant when his or her request is reasonable. Reasonable includes buying a new or secondhand refrigerator when the appliance in a unit own stops functioning, replacing a dishwasher when it rinses the dishes but doesn't dry them, fixing or replacing stove, replacing damaged floor tiles or linoleum when warranted, painting the apartment regularly, or promptly replacing broken controls, faucets or shower heads in the kitchen or bathroom. My new tenant, Miss Lucy Lukiless, was a sweetheart and not bad looking to boot. She always called me when she had the rent and had the courtesy to let me know if she didn't, always informing me how long I'd have to wait.

Lucy asked me for a new refrigerator. Between you and me, if she also had asked me for a new stove, I'd have thrown it in too, even if the one she had was in good shape. A good tenant should be treated well. As I mentioned before, the majority of my tenants are good people. I wouldn't survive without them. I could have fixed her refrigerator but instead opted to buy her a new one. The new fridge was supposedly shipped on a Tuesday to her duplex home at 18-23 40th Road. But four days later, she still hadn't received the refrigerator. The dispatcher said that her address was on the Tuesday delivery list, and the two deliverymen swore they had delivered it.

"Somebody signed for it," the driver said. "I have all the receipts, even though the signature on my copy is not clear. Somebody definitely signed for it at that address."

Meanwhile, Lucy had to throw away a lot of spoiled food. I bought her a secondhand small refrigerator until the mess was unraveled. Instead of the dispatcher admitting that maybe his drivers delivered it to the wrong address and the wrong person had accepted it, he chose to believe the deliverymen. I was rapidly getting tired of hearing stories and was ready to take legal action. Lucy's patience was also wearing thin. She was ready to break someone's neck and I hoped it wasn't mine. Meanwhile, Lucy received a bill to pay for the missing refrigerator. She was so angry that I had to restrain her. I was just as angry, but knew it wouldn't help to display it. I wrote two strong letters to the appliance store, warning them that if Lucy didn't get her refrigerator in the next couple days, I would sue them. Two days later, I received a reply that the dispatcher would honor my request and allow me to accompany the drivers on their route, providing they would agree, and there was enough room in the truck for me to sit. Drivers Manny Mindliss and Joe Cluliss had no objections. While we started on our way, I told them that maybe I could jog their memory where they delivered the missing frig, or where it is if they suddenly remembered that they forgot to deliver it? They didn't respond. When 40th Road was directly ahead, I told Manny to turn right and stop at Lucy's house. As I suspected, neither of them recognized the house. I had a thought: maybe they had delivered the refrigerator to the right address number but the wrong street. I asked Manny to keep driving. The next block was 40th Lane. I told him to stop in front of 18-23 40th Lane. Again, they didn't recognize the house. I started feeling that my brilliant idea was worthless, but when Manny drove one more block and pulled up to 18-23 40th *Street*, my idea suddenly turned to gold.

Joe Cluliss hollered out, "Don't you remember, Manny, we delivered a fridge to this house two weeks ago?"

"You're right, Billy; I completely forgot."

Manny and I walked up the steps to the front door and rang the bell.

A humungous specimen of a man opened the door. "What do you guys want? I'm in the middle of lunch, and when I'm hungry, I don't like to be disturbed."

I don't know what Mindliss was thinking, but this guy scared the crap out of me. I was debating whether I should forget about the lousy refrigerator, or take the chance that he'd kill me. My choice was obvious. I had to be a man and live up to my promise to Lucy.

Mindliss returned to the truck, probably figuring his job was over. I gathered my strength, and cleared my throat.

"I'm sorry to bother you sir, I said. "But I think you may have received a refrigerator that was meant for someone else." I held my breath and tensed my whole body, praying that he wouldn't pick me up and fling me someplace.

But surprisingly, he replied calmly in a polite tone of voice. "Yes sir, I do remember my sister signing for a refrigerator a couple weeks ago. But unfortunately, she's in Europe now and I can't really help you until she returns in two weeks."

"Oh, that's a shame" I said. "I was hoping that she left behind a copy of the delivery receipt and you'd be able to show it to me. That way, I could tell if the refrigerator you received was meant for this address and not delivered here by mistake."

"I fully understand and would like to help you as much as I can," he said. "She keeps all her bills and stuff in one of the back rooms. Let me look back there. Maybe I'll find something."

Anxiously awaiting his return, I asked myself what I'd do if the sister's name were also Lucy. C'mon, Carlos, so what if there are two Lucy's? What are the odds they'd have the same last name? Ten minutes later, Mr. Humongous returned with all the answers. The receipt was made out to Lucy Lukiless, residing at 18-23 40th Road. The signature at the bottom read "Lucy Lukiless."

But there was one problem; it wasn't Lucy's signature. Mr. Humongous didn't pay any attention to the receipt when he handed it to me, which was a stroke of luck. His sister had forged a signature and accepted something not belonging to her.

Humongous, without asking any questions let me make a photocopy of the receipt, never looking at the original before putting it back in the drawer. I thanked him for his cooperation and went back to the delivery truck. As far as I was concerned, Humongous, his sister, and Lucy's fridge could all live together as one happy family forever and ever. I called the appliance store and gave all the proof they needed to clear Lucy's name, and I personally monitored the shipping of the new one. Lucy received it the same day. What's the moral of the story? Give the money to the tenants and let them buy their own damn refrigerator.

CHAPTER EIGHTEEN

MISS DECEPTION

I HAVE NEVER LIKED using real estate brokers. They have a lousy track record with me. It's probably because tenants in my area are poor people who can barely pay one month's rent and one month's security to move in. Paying one month's commission to a broker on top of that is simply too much for them.

Miss Deception came through a broker. She was an attractive woman in her thirties, and except for her two missing teeth, made a positive impression. Quite frankly, when I think about it, she was a goddess compared to most of my problem tenants. The broker and I both remarked on how even though the interview went well, she never made eye contact. That never sits well with me. We checked her out from top to bottom and side-to-side, not thinking for a second that an inside out look was also necessary. That oversight turned out to be a huge mistake.

For the next three months, everything was fine. Miss Deception paid me on the first of each month, never complaining about a thing. In the middle of the third month, just by chance, I met the broker on the street and complimented her for sending me such a wonderful tenant. But in the fourth month, things changed. Miss Deception said she was having financial problems, and needed more time to pay the rent.

"About how long would that be?" I asked.

"Next month I'll pay you for two months," she said.

I bought her promise, another huge mistake. A week or two later I heard that a man had moved in with her. *But so what?* I asked myself. Why should I have cared? This indifference proved to be another mistake. On the first day of the fifth month, I knocked on Miss Deception's door. She was half-dressed with lacerations on her forearm and bruises above the eye.

"What happened to you?" I asked.

Breaking down in tears, she told me that her ex had beat her up and taken all the rent money. I started smelling trouble, not even asking when she would resume paying. What my perfect tenant failed to add was that her ex was a druggie who owed lots of money to some unsavory individuals.

Wasting no time, I served her with a thirty-day notice, knowing from my limited experience that it might take months to evict her. A couple of days after she received the notice, all hell broke loose. The next-door neighbor called me at home, ranting and babbling so fast that I could barely understand her.

"I hear a woman screaming and it doesn't stop. It's definitely from your building next door," the neighbor said. "You better come right away."

I hurried over. Inside the apartment, Miss Deception's ex was throwing things against the wall. When she tried to stop him, he sliced her cheek with a sharp instrument. He told me to get lost or I'd get the same. There was no doubt he was serious. I closed the door and called 911. Ten minutes later, an ambulance and two police cars were on the scene. The cops saw everything I did and told me privately that there was nothing they could do, saying it was a family dispute and as long as no one was in danger, there was nothing for the police to do.

"Go home, mister, and leave these people alone," one of the cops said.

"Did I hear you correctly?" I asked them. Blood was dripping from Mrs. Deception's face onto the floor.

"Yes," he said. "And if you don't lower your voice, I'll haul you off to the station."

As the cops were about to leave, I approached their car, and asked one of them to roll down the window because I had something to tell them.

"Mark my word officers. Murder is on the horizon."

They completely ignored me and drove off.

The second day of the following month, while on the way to Miss Deception's building to collect the rent, I decided to visit my wife, who had a boutique a half-mile away. While shooting the breeze with her, we both heard a man that we knew hollering in the distance.

"*Julio muerte, Julio muerte,*" he shouted. The second the man entered the store, we saw he was shaking like a leaf. He talked so fast it was almost impossible to understand him. But we managed to hear him say that three guys had entered Mrs. Deception's room where Julio her husband was sleeping and all three pumped bullets into him while he was asleep. As the killers fled, Miss. Deception, kitchen knife in hand, chased after them. Just as she caught up with them, one of the killers spun around and slashed her arm with his knife. But she managed to stab him in the back as he entered his car. Four police cars and one ambulance were on the scene in a flash, rushing Miss Deception, bleeding profusely, to the hospital. The police barricaded the area and questioned everyone in sight. Where was I? A zillion miles away, not anxious to have the police include me in their investigation. Surprisingly, they never contacted me. My wife, a real trooper, helped me clean the apartment. This was a job that I wouldn't wish on my worst enemy. Two weeks later, we rented the studio to a married Latino couple. Two years later, the husband became the super for two of my other buildings. I'm happy to say, he's still with me.

CHAPTER NINETEEN

THE INTERNET CAFE

I KNOW SEVERAL LANDLORDS who have rented spaces to an Internet cafe business. None of them had a problem collecting rent. Internet cafés had just recently become popular, and every one and his brother were curious to check them out. They were basically a room full of computers connected to the Internet. People could pay to use the computers by the hour.

On the second floor of one of my commercial buildings, I had some empty space suitable for this kind of business. The second floor is always difficult to rent, so a landlord can't afford to be too fussy, or the space could remain empty for a long time. One day, a young Asian man (we'll refer to him as Nicky Notinky) answered my ad. He asked me if he could rent the space for an Internet cafe.

This was music to my ears. What could be better than a trouble-free, reliable tenant? Notinky said that he worked for someone that owned an Internet cafe and felt he could start a new one on his own. He made an excellent impression on me, but for a change, I was smart, asking him for many references, which included his mother and former boss. To be even more thorough, I requested seeing more than three pieces of ID. What more could I do, other than run a profile check through Interpol? He checked out and signed a lease. The next day he brought in eight computers and desks to put them on. He also built a large wooden stand for serving nonalcoholic beverages and sandwiches. At the time, I was pretty much an idiot when it came to computers. I'm proud to say I have since graduated to a mere moron. But my lack of knowledge proved costly back then. I had absolutely no idea that one could access websites containing extreme violence and pornography. I also didn't know that my reputable new tenant depended on those kinds of websites to make a living. Every day, between ten and twenty teenage punks bought time slots and, on more than one occasion, acted out their rage, smashing chairs into the snack bar or tossing them at the windows. Once they broke a pane of glass, but luckily, the opening wasn't large enough for the chair to go through and land on somebody's head. Every day or two, somebody defecated on the bathroom floor, leaving it for someone else to remove. One or more of them were constantly spreading graffiti all over the walls, including in the hallway.

I was damned sure that my interview with Mr. Notinky had covered all the bases. But like they say, only three things are sure in this world: birth, death and taxes. I failed to take into consideration whether or not he was a take-charge guy. If he was, all the damage could have been avoided. After two or three months of this torture, I asked Notinky to leave, having only waited that long because he cleaned the place daily and constantly apologized. The final straw was when a half-drunk punk barged into a doctor's office on the same floor and started spewing profanity. Three patients couldn't handle it and walked out. When I heard this, I sent Nicky Notinky packing. Maybe one day he'll start thinking. He felt so bad that he paid someone to scrub the walls, remove all the graffiti, change the broken window, and machine-polish the entire floor. Even though he caused me a lot of grief, I respected him for being decent and not leaving me to do all the dirty work myself.

CHAPTER TWENTY

THE TAX ABATEMENT

TAX ABATEMENT IS A city agency incentive program that grants an exemption or reduction of taxes to local businesses for a specified period in order to stimulate the economy by providing jobs and affordable housing. In my case, a relatively simple process of submitting an application showing eligibility to receive tax abatement and have it approved by the city echelon turned into a nightmare.

In the mid eighties, while on vacation in a large Midwestern city, I spotted a huge empty lot that interested me. The lot was zoned for residential, but situated in a very busy commercial area. The price was so ridiculously cheap that I couldn't pass it up. The owners held the mortgage. The zoning allowed me to construct a twenty-four-family apartment building with four garages. At the time, building materials were cheap and jobs were scarce, so plenty of nonunion men were willing to work for less-than-union wages. This allowed me to afford hiring a reputable architect and construction company.

Billie Dallier, a lawyer specializing in obtaining real-estate tax abatement's for his clients, took my down payment for his services and filled out the application forms required to be eligible for consideration. The following day, he went to the fifth floor of the city building, an office dealing only with tax abatement processing, and submitted the forms to a clerk at the window. Their policy was not to give receipts. When he returned to his office without one, I was bewildered as to why he didn't get a receipt. He said it was standard policy and there was nothing he could do to change things. Four months passed. Nothing. Six months. Still nothing. Now I started getting ants in the pants.

"Mr. Dallier, could you please check on our status?"

Dallier replied, "You remember in the beginning, I told you these things take time? You can't hurry them. We're dealing with a city agency. Do I have to say more?"

I knew he was right but nevertheless, he should have heard something. I let two more months pass, but that was it. My lawyer was sitting on his dead ass doing nothing, so I decided to continue on my own. All tax-related offices were situated in a huge thirty-eight floor building in the down town area. When you first entered, you had to talk to a security guard. If you didn't pass an oral test, he wouldn't let you through.

I didn't have a name of who I was visiting and I didn't have a floor I was headed to. The name board listed four different tax-related offices, but nothing about tax abatements. Each of the four offices was on a different floor. The only way I could get upstairs was to improvise, so I lied to the guard, telling him I was here to see Mrs. Brown from the tax abatement office, but I wasn't sure that was her name. He said that I couldn't go up without an appointment.

Plan A hadn't worked, so I tried plan B. "Sir, I see that I'll have to do as you say and make an appointment, but do me a favor. Since I'm here, tell me which floor to go to for income tax forms?" This didn't require seeing a specific person, so he gave me permission to go up. I needed tax forms like I needed a hole in my head. I simply wanted to know which floor the tax abatement office was on. I grabbed a few forms and asked one of the lady clerks if she happened to know where the tax abatement office was.

"One floor up," she said. "But you're not allowed in there."

I ignored her warning and took the elevator to the next floor. The minute I walked into the abatement office, a charming elderly lady stopped me and asked what I wanted. I told her that I had made an appointment with, I believe, a Mrs. Brown but didn't see her anywhere. This was another lie.

"I'm sorry," the kindly woman said. "This office is off limits to the public, so I must ask you to leave."

There was no way that I was going to leave. I didn't have a plan C, but I was pretty good at thinking fast on my feet. I knew if I could find a way to capture her attention, she might let me explain my plight.

"I filed for tax abatement eight months ago," I said, before she had a chance to open her mouth. "But nobody has the application or knows of its existence. Please, you must help me. My lawyer set me back eight months and I'm afraid I'll lose the building."

Suddenly she changed her tune. The chemistry between us helped a lot.

"Wait here," she said. "I'll be right back."

I stood there for fifteen minutes waiting for something to happen. Eventually a huge man with a cane walked toward me with my elderly helper right behind him.

"What is your name, sir?" he asked.

"You can call me Mr. Carlos," I said.

"I'm told your application is lost. Is that true?"

"Yes sir," I answered. "Well, I am going to make an exception," he said. "I'm going to help you, but don't mention this to anyone. If the director hears how I am circumventing normal procedure, she'll have my head on a plate, and serve it to both of us for dinner. First thing I want to do is see what happened to your application. It couldn't just disappear into thin air. Wait in my office. I'll be back in a few minutes."

A half hour later he returned with a vexed look on his face. "I found your application, Mr. Carlos. It was in a drawer marked 'Rejection.'"

"How can that be, sir?"

"I looked there," he replied, "only because it was the last possible place it could be, other than the garbage. When an application is denied, he continued, the clerk puts it, temporarily, in the rejection drawer until the time comes to dispose of it. Apparently, some careless person shoved it in there without looking at it."

I was steaming, but this man was going out of his way to help me so I restrained myself.

"What do we do next?" I asked.

He told me to write a letter to the director explaining my plight, but not to say anything about his discovering the application. "Here's some paper. Start writing!" he said. "I will advise you what to say. But remember, I am only advising you, not telling you. You won't have to fill out any forms or questionnaires. The only thing you need to do is find a notary to authenticate your signature. Once the letter is ready, I'll take it directly to the big boss for approval. Your old application will find its way to the garbage. You understand? It doesn't exist."

"I understand perfectly," I said. We sat together for almost an hour before we were both satisfied that I had dotted all the I's and crossed all the T's. My savior was going on vacation the following day, so it was imperative that I find a notary right away.

A $300 inducement was all it took to get a notary up to the tax abatement office on short notice. I signed the letter, and the notary put his seal on it. As promised, my savior took the letter to the big boss. Two weeks later, I received my official tax abatement certificate in the mail. I have guarded it with my life ever since.

CHAPTER TWENTY-ONE

THE TRAP DOOR

USUALLY A BUILDING INSPECTOR will not discover a violation unless someone calls the building department to complain. The following story is a perfect example of how this works.

One day, my tenant, Mr. Selfdoo, called me to his store. He said that a building department inspector was there acting on a complaint and had asked to see the large hole that someone carved out in the floor. Onisown reluctantly led him to a corner in the back of the store and removed a pile of assorted boxes, exposing a large hole in the floor. Just as I arrived, I saw the inspector looking at the hole. He took out his book and wrote up a summons, naming me as the guilty party. Selfdoo had carved out the hole so his workers and deliverymen could throw heavy boxes of clothing down to the basement and avoid carrying the boxes down the long flight of stairs. My tenant never told me that he planned to carve out this hole. We both had personal liability policies. But what would happen if some careless worker fell through the hole and died? I don't even want to think about it. The summons read that I had to close the hole and return the floor to its original condition, pay a $500 fine, mail in a certificate of correction, and appear in court on the specified date.

I saw how difficult it was for Mr. Selfdoo to take merchandise to the basement without the hole so I thought of an alternative. We could build a trap door with a latch, kept secure with a padlock when not in use. I asked the inspector if I could do this.

He said that he didn't see why not but told me to hire an architect to submit plans to the building department for approval. I did what he told me but didn't have patience to wait for the anticipated approval. So I went ahead and built the trap door. I filled out a certificate of correction, coupled with a letter explaining, in detail, the steps I took to comply with the directives, the date the work was completed, and whom I hired to do the work. I put all the original paperwork in a large manila envelope, also enclosing photos that I took from every conceivable angle, and mailed the envelope via certified mail

Two weeks passed and I didn't have any response from the building department. Another week passed; still no word. My patience was wearing thin so I called them for answers. A Miss Shaffter told me that they never received a thing from me

"How can that be? I asked. I mailed the letter three weeks ago."

"I'm sorry sir," she said. "We never got it."

Now I was in deep defecation. I missed the first court date and got permission for a new one. Thank God I had made copies, but it was too late to mail them a duplicate set. I didn't want to take the chance the building department would also lose this set. My only option was bringing the copies to ECB court and showing them directly to the judge. Administrative Judge Steinway with an ass as big as a Wurlitzer and the building department representative Miss Spinet with an ass as big as two Wurlitzer's, joined me in the hearing room.

I showed the judge all the papers, emphasizing the small white receipt the post office had given me for my lost application when I mailed it in. I explained to her all that had happened, from the time of the first mailing to the present. After scanning the copies, not paying attention to detail, Judge Steinway shook her head.

"Nothing you showed me is sufficient proof that you mailed it here. The white receipt the post office gave you is not convincing. You could write any address you want on it. The post office doesn't care. It's your copy." She turned to Miss Spinet "What do you think we should do? she asked.

It was Miss Spinet's turn to weigh in. "I agree with you judge, but even if we received these papers, it would still have been rejected, because the certificate of correction form is obsolete. The logo is on the left side. The new forms have the logo on the right side. And most important, these are copies. We can only accept originals."

I couldn't take it anymore. I was ready to erupt. At this point, I didn't give a damn what these two fatsos did to me. "Judge, this is the most ridiculous thing I ever heard. Are you honestly going to allow these technicalities to take precedence?" I asked.

The judge turned back to Miss Spinet. "I believe Mr. Carlos is right," she said. "What do you suggest we do with this man?"

"Impose a mitigating fine of $250, "It's possible that he's telling the truth."

"So be it," the judge said. "Mr. Carlos, you will receive my decision in the mail. And keep in mind, sir; you have to mail the building department an original certificate of correction. No copies."

Now I was *really* pissed off. "Your honor," I said, "I see that you already made your decision. Why don't you give me the bill now and we'll get it over with? Oh, one more thing, your honor. For arguments sake, if had mailed the certificate of correction return receipt requested and the recipient's signature was not legible, would that also be considered insufficient proof?"

The judge ignored my comment and left the room without even saying good-bye. Boy, did I get reamed. Not only did I have to pay $500 at the outset, but now, another $250. All this because I wanted to be the good guy and help my tenant. What's that expression? Nice guys finish last?

This wasn't even the end of it. I had to make a set of copies of the originals that I would mail in so I would have what I needed for another court appearance, in case the building department didn't receive my new certificate of correction before the next scheduled court date. Just my luck, the building department didn't get my certificate of correction in time. It's a good thing I made copies to show the judge.

Judge Smakur was a mean-looking bastard. He looked to be about seven feet tall, and that's when he was seated. I stood alone before him, awaiting the first assault.

"Mr. Carlos, sir, can I see your proof of compliance?"

"Yes, your honor," I said as I approached the bench. I handed him an envelope containing everything the building department demanded, but nothing showing that the architect's plans were approved. The judge concentrated more on my photos of the trap door than on anything else. When he finished perusing, he looked up at me, staring directly into my eyes for several seconds.

"Mr. Carlos, did you read that the citation explicitly states you are to completely close the hole? A trap door can be opened. That is not compliance, sir. You will receive my decision in the mail. Case dismissed"

Two weeks later, the decision arrived. My mouth opened to its fullest extent. I had to pay a $4,000 fine within thirty days, bringing the total to $4,750, and was put on record as falsifying a certificate of correction because I swore that I had 'completely' closed the hole in the floor. In my judgment, a trap door, closed securely with a minimum of space on all four sides, is in no way dangerous. Otherwise, why would trap doors exist? To make a long story short, I disassembled the trap door and restored the floor to its original condition. Now I could add fabricating to my list of misconducts. I'm already a car thief and a procurer. I was ready to swallow the first two fines, totaling $750, but when they nailed me with an additional $4,000, I decided it was time for my tenant to make a contribution. He reluctantly reimbursed me $2,000. It was less than I wanted, but better than nothing. A month later, I was explaining to another landlord my miserable experience when he suddenly interrupted me.

"Schmuck, on that little white receipt is a tracking number. With that number, you could have called the post office to learn where your package was delivered or if it got lost."

At this point, to pursue the matter served no purpose except to satisfy my curiosity. I took my landlord friend's advice and called the post office with the tracking number. Guess what? My package was delivered to the building department and signed for by a Jeremy Loosett. My blood was boiling. Now it wasn't just curiosity driving me but anger as well. I had to find out where in the building department this moron worked or die trying.

The building department office consisted of six floors, each one bustling with activity. Men and women were running up and down steps carrying huge stacks of paper. Tough-looking inspectors with ostentatious metal badges attached to a string around their necks strutted around like peacocks in the hallways. Landlords banged their fists on copy machines that swallowed their money. Employees banged their fists on soda machines that swallowed their money. Janitors were busy mopping the soapy, wet floor, so everyone had an equal chance to slip and break their neck. JeremyLoosett, if he existed, had to be working in either a mailroom or shipping and receiving area. If I wanted to find this guy, I, couldn't tell anyone working there the real reason I was looking for him. It was certain they would cover for him. I had to come up with a phony story, and equally important, had to ask the right person to get the right answers. My first move was making sure there was somebody there named Jeremy Loosett and pray that he didn't change his name to duck creditors or escape paying alimony. I went straight to the information desk, hoping the clerk would help me.

she looked through some papers and said that she was sorry but there was no record of a Jeremy Loosett.

"That can't be," I said. "He's been working here for at least a year." I made that up.

"Sir, don't get snotty with me. If you feel that I have not provided you with outstanding service, you can request to speak to a supervisor."

Boy, do I cringe when I hear those words.

I asked the supervisor, Miss Moredum, the same question that I asked the first dummy. No luck. I decided to go to the back of the building where the mailroom and receiving section were located. When I got there, I ran into a problem. Two security guards blocked the entranceway, refusing to let me pass. That did it. I had enough. There was no point in pursuing the matter. Even if I did find the dickhead, it was too late to do anything. But just as I was turning around to exit the building, I had a sudden brainstorm. Maybe one of these two guards knew the guy. What could I lose by asking?

John Fingerman rubbed his chin for a moment. "Jeremy, yeah, I know him. He works in that back room with six other guys. They sort out packages and large envelopes shipped here via UPS or Federal Express. Jimmy also knows the guy. Right, Jimmy?"

His shrimp partner nodded his assent.

"What do you want with him?" Fingerman asked.

"I met him at a party last week," I answered, "and we hit it off so good he told me if I ever was going to the building department, to call him at home the night before and he'd meet me here. The problem is that I lost his telephone number."

"You want me to call him out here?" Fingerman asked. "Nah," I responded. "It's getting late. But do me a favor and tell him I was here. If he wants, he can call me. He has my number."

"Okay, I will," he said.

I had my answer, what would I do next? You guessed it: zero.

CHAPTER TWENTY-TWO

DOCTOR NOTREW

I ONCE RENTED A fully furnished three-bedroom apartment to a Doctor Notrew, a gynecologist and his wife. They were two recent immigrants that came here to make a fresh start. I tried very hard not to omit anything important in the interview. I asked to see ID, two references, applicable licenses and, equally important, asked them why they left their country to come here.

The certificate that the doctor showed me was only good in Guatemala, his country of origin. He said that he had already submitted an application to practice in New York and was sure that within a week, it would be approved. Mrs. Notrew said her husband was seeing fewer and fewer patients in Guatemala but she was sure it would be different in the United States.

About one month into their lease, I ran into Maria, a former tenant of mine, also from Guatemala, standing at a bus stop near my apartment. After engaging in some small talk with her, I asked if by chance she knew a Dr. Notrew.

"Pedro Notrew?" she asked.

"I don't know his first name," I said, "but I can describe him to you."

Upon hearing my description, she confirmed that it was the same Notrew she knew of. "Yeah, that's him," she said. "I can't tell you anything for sure, only rumors. I heard that he had a big underground abortion clinic in a village just outside the capital and about two months ago, he botched an abortion, resulting in a mother-to-Be's death. The way I heard it," she continued, "they took away his license. That's probably the reason he came to this country."

Yet another thorough interviewing job by me had led to trouble. I had to know whether all that Maria told me was true. I didn't have the patience to wait for an answer so I headed straight to his apartment. He was having dinner with his wife, and invited me to join them.

I asked him for the truth, point blank. "Did you have your license taken away in Guatemala?"

"Who told you that?" he asked. "Of course not. Otherwise, how could I apply for a new one here and be approved?"

"Makes sense," I replied. "But you realize, doctor, I still have to ask these questions. I just can't ignore the rumors that I heard. He appeared to understand. I apologized for the intrusion and as I was about to leave, I smelled something like alcohol coming from one of the bedrooms near the front door. The bedroom door was partially open, permitting the strong odor to find its way directly to my nostrils. Curious to know its source, I asked the doctor's permission to go inside

"I'm sorry, Mr. Carlos. My son is getting dressed. You'll have to wait a few minutes."

A realization dawned on me. "What son? You never said anything about a son. I'm sorry, doctor, but I have to see what's in that bedroom, so stand aside."

I couldn't believe what I saw. There was a six-foot-long table covered with a white sheet and padding underneath. There were bloodstains on parts of the sheet. On top of a small table resting against the wall were sutures, small pliers, and two pairs of scissors. These two bastards had played me! I had a clinic under my nose.

"Doctor," I said, "if you want to run an abortion clinic, it's your choice, but I'll be damned if I'll let you conduct business in my apartment, and especially without a license. I want you and your so-called nurse to get out of here pronto. Otherwise, I won't wait for a date in the landlord tenant court. I have my own ways to get you out. I'll make sure, with the cooperation of the district attorney that it'll happen within a week. Be smart. Save yourself a lot of pain. Just leave!"

Exactly two days later, he completely emptied the apartment, returning it to me in tip-top condition, never saying a word while I stood watching the movers load up his belongings. As soon as they finished loading the truck, the disgraced doctor left. Hopefully, he and his wife, or who ever she was, had left the area for good. This experience taught me a valuable lesson. Background checks should include hiring a $300-an-hour private investigator. In this case, it would have been damn well worth it.

CHAPTER TWENTY-THREE

THE LIGHT SWITCH

ONE BLUSTERY, COLD DAY in December, a restaurant owner in a building that I haven't mentioned before, who had his own separate heating system, told me that one of my four residential tenants had complained to him that he didn't have heat. There were plenty of possible explanations: a faulty thermostat, bad wires, not enough water in the boiler, too much water in the boiler, the black start-up switch on the boiler in the off position, the red emergency switch on the wall leading to the basement in the off position, or not enough oil in the tank causing sludge to build up in the lines.

The first thing I did was having an electrician check that all the thermostats were on and the wires were connected correctly. The electrician said that he couldn't find what the problem was so I let him go. Maybe the heat coils in the boiler had burnt out, rendering it permanently useless. Meanwhile, the residential tenants in all four apartments were screaming they didn't have heat and called city hot lines to complain. I was added to the city's list of abusive landlords. The city is not interested in reasons why the tenant has no heat, only in results.

A tenant named Mr. Thresher called. He told me in no uncertain terms that if either of his two kids got sick as a result of the lack of heat, he'd stick me with the doctor bills. "I'm giving you exactly twenty-four hours to get me heat. If you don't, you'll soon see my lawyer Mr. Scrumore."

Vinnie Nuttworth, a licensed plumber and very good friend of my best friend, was on the scene in five minutes, an unusual feat in the wintertime. Promptness always gains my respect. I was sure he'd get the boiler started. Nutworth checked everything I did, even though I told him not to bother. He took out some tools from his bag and started tightening and loosening several boiler attachments. An hour later, he dropped his tools on the floor and looked at me with a defeated expression on his face.

"I'm sorry, Mr. Carlos, I can't help you. Maybe you should consider buying a new boiler. I can get you one dirt cheap."

"No thanks," I said. "I'll figure out something and let you know." I just wanted to get rid of him. I paid him his $50 for the two hours of play and sent him on his merry way. I was back to square one, and under the gun to find someone with a whole brain, not half. There were only twelve hours left before I'd have the pleasure of meeting Attorney Scrumore. Suddenly I remembered this plumber called Mr. Magic. He was a troubleshooter that no one hired unless they had a complex problem that a regular plumber couldn't solve. It took me a while to find him. He was said to be the best of the best, so I hoped that a solution was just around the corner.

Mr. Magic told me he'd be there in ten minutes. He was there in twenty, but that's okay. The last guy came right away. Look where that got me? I explained to Mr. Magic what the previous plumber had checked, double-checked, and triple checked. Mr. Magic didn't care. He was not ready to accept the findings of another plumber. The Magic man charged $200 an hour. But you get what you pay for, right? Unfortunately, three hours and $600 later, after double-checking and triple checking, he threw up his hands.

"I am really sorry, sir. I've tried *everything* and nothing works. You should consider calling the manufacturer to send a troubleshooter. Maybe there's something he can do. If not, demand a new boiler."

The so-called Magic Man was just as useless as the last plumber. The only difference between them was the rate they charged. Mr. Magic, or whatever the dummy's real name was, apologized for not being able to get the boiler working, but still charged me $200, reminding me that he had told me up front that I would have to pay for his time regardless of results.

"But you can't charge me so much when you didn't fix a rotten thing," I said.

"Okay, mister; just give me $100."

Even that was too much, but I saw it wouldn't do any good to argue. I gave him his lousy $100. As he approached the exit, he spun around and hollered at me.

"Where's my tip? I worked my butt off trying to solve your problem!"

"Tip?" I said angrily. "Get your sorry, tired ass out of here pronto. I don't need your phony magic."

He huffed and puffed, slamming the door behind him. All I needed now was bursting pipes and water damage to make the day complete. Hiring another boiler technician would be stupid. My warrantee on the boiler was expired, so I opted to buy a whole new boiler. While waiting for the new boiler to be installed, I put a few electric heaters in each apartment at my expense. After informing the tenants that a new boiler would arrive in three days, they all calmed down a bit, including Thretzer. Three days later, just as I was promised, the boiler arrived. I hired a guy who worked for the same company that supplied me oil to install it on his own time.

Are we finally finished? I'm afraid not. We're just getting started. Johnny Onkaul, the technician, finished installing the boiler, and as he stood up to stretch his legs, gave me a wink. I winked back and flipped the switch to start the boiler. Guess what? It didn't start. Johnny double-checked to make sure all the wiring was done correctly and that none of the attached parts were defective. We looked at one another and instantly reached the same conclusion: It had to be an electrical problem.

I gave Johnny a few hundred dollars, thanked him for installing the boiler, and sent him home. My next move should have been calling the nearest mental hospital to come take me away. Now I was in the middle of the creek without a boat or a paddle, and a storm was brewing and I didn't even have a raincoat. My tenants were chewing their nails and ready to chew on me. I didn't have a clue what to do. I couldn't keep paying for the heaters in their apartment much longer, and didn't have the guts to tell them the truth, especially Thretzer. I returned home, feeling helpless as a fly in a spiderweb.

The following morning, I went back to the torture scene with absolutely no idea what to do. But because I have strong belief in God, I was certain he'd find a way to save me; never realizing how soon deliverance might come. While I stood near the boiler daydreaming, the restaurant owner asked me to do him a favor and bring some plates up. It was no big deal; I put the plates in a box and started up the stairs. In keeping with my luck, I stumbled near the top of the landing, falling smack into the panel box containing the red emergency switch for the boiler which should be in the up position at all times, and a black switch in the off position that was for a rarely used storage room. No body bothered to change the light bulbs in that room for at least a month. As I fell into the panel box, I accidentally flipped the black switch up to the on position.

Just like that, the boiler kicked in. You heard me correctly. That stupid, no-good, son-of-a-bitch boiler started running.

Later I told the whole story to Vinnie Nuttworth.

He laughed. "I think I know what happened. The day your tenant complained to me that he had no heat was the same day two of my guys painted walls in the basement, banisters, parts of the ceiling, and the panel box containing the emergency switch. Most of the red paint on the emergency switch had peeled off. I bet the painter probably painted it black by mistake."

This stupid mistake almost cost me my sanity, not to mention the money I spent on brilliant technicians and a brand-new boiler. I hope I never run into that idiot painter, or I may be incarcerated for painting him black and blue for all to view.

CHAPTER TWENTY-FOUR

THE SQUATTERS

ONE SUMMER, MY WIFE and her girlfriend went on a ten-day vacation to Florida. Just prior to leaving, without my knowledge, my wife rented out 450 square feet of commercial space to the eighteen-year-old son of her beautician. I didn't know her beautician or the beautician's son. I had no clue what he was going to do in the space or how long my wife had allowed him to do it. I seldom went near that property, because it had been empty for over a year and was located in a dangerous neighborhood.

But when I heard from a lady tenant of mine living a block away that excessive noise was coming from the property at all hours of the day and night, I went to see who was causing the ruckus. On top of the entry was a sign reading "Social Club, All Welcome." I peered through the window and saw a half-dozen men and women dancing to music blasting from a jukebox. In one corner were four men playing cards and two or three women playing what appeared to be a video poker machine. On a scale from one to ten, the noise level was eleven.

I banged on the door, identifying myself as the building owner. A rough and shabby-looking teen opened the door and asked me what I wanted. I told him that I didn't care how he got into the place but just to get the hell out. The kid identified himself as the son of my wife's beautician and said that my wife gave him permission to be there until she returned from her vacation. My blood pressure was quickly rising to the roof. What's your name, kid? I asked. "Johnny", he said. "Listen to me, young man," I said. "I don't care what arrangements you made with my wife. I'm the owner of this building and I make the rules here. I want every body out of here by tomorrow morning. And until then, you tell the others to keep the noise down or I'll call the police." Another kid overheard my warning and stepped forward. "Listen, old man, your wife told Johnny that we could use this place until she came back from her trip. We ain't doing nuttin' wrong, so you can't talk to us like dat. She knew that we had a jukebox so she had to know that there'd be noise. I saw that booting all those troublemakers out was not going to be easy.

By this time, everybody in the place was gabbing away. The music from the jukebox was so damn loud that I couldn't make out what anybody was saying. There was only one-way to get these squatters out: I had to call the cops immediately, not wait for the morning. But there were no guarantees that they'd help me. They usually stay clear of landlord tenant disputes. It was getting late and the cops took their sweet-ass time showing up. About eleven-thirty P.M. a police car pulled up to the curb. Out came two male policemen and one female officer. Before they went inside the store they motioned me to the side.

"Sir, can you tell us exactly why we're here?" Officer Dubyus asked me.

The excessive noise didn't seem to faze him. I briefed him as best I could.

He asked me if the squatters had a lease.

I reminded him that my wife had put them in the place, not me. But as far as I knew, there was no lease.

The second policeman, an Officer Longwith, told me I couldn't evict them by force unless I proved they had moved in without permission. "It looks like your wife is the only one that can help us determine that."

Once the four of us were inside the store, Officer Dubyus asked to speak to the person claiming to have my wife's permission to be there.

Johnny stepped forward. "I am, sir." My mother owns a beauty parlor a few blocks from here.

Officer Dubyus turned toward me. "I'm sorry, mister, our hands are tied. We have to wait for your wife to return." He turned to address the group. "You guys better keep the noise down or we'll have to come back here and issue you a summons."

No one said a word, but as the officers exited, I asked them if at least they could give me a copy of the key in the event of an emergency.

"That's a landlord-tenant matter. We're not allowed to get involved," Officer Dubyus, responded.

The female officer named Sidewyth, who had yet to open her mouth, turned to Johnny. "This man should have a set of keys. He's the landlord. So why don't you give him copies?"

The two male officers pretended they hadn't heard and returned to the car.

Officer Sidewyth quietly pressed the issue. "If you don't want me back here every day, you give this man a set of keys. You understand me?" she growled at Johnny.

Without further ado, Johnny reached under the counter of the bar and handed the officer a set of keys. On the way out, she turned around and winked at me, handing me the keys.

"Don't you dare say anything about this," she said. "I could get into a lot of trouble."

I winked back and told her not to worry. God bless that Officer Sidewyth. I took my set of keys and left without saying good-bye to the squatters. I decided to leave the punks alone. I knew that it wouldn't be for long.

At seven A.M. the next morning, while the squatters were asleep, I changed the locks on the outside gate of the social club. The squatters could have run to the police and told them what I did, but I took the chance they wouldn't. My wife was coming back in less than a week. That was hardly enough time for the wheels of justice to run their course and legally force me to let the punks back in. As I suspected, no one from the club opened their mouth to the cops. I couldn't wait to confront my wife. When I picked her up at the airport, I laid it all out for her.

She wasn't fazed by my outburst. "Dear," she said, "Johnny is the son of my beautician. She asked me if her son could use the store for a recording studio until I returned."

"My darling, your musical maestro and the other ten maestros did not use the place for a recording studio. They used it for a hard-rock concert hall. The noise was so deafening I had to call the cops to get them out." I didn't tell her that I had changed the lock five days ago.

"So what's so terrible?" she asked. "They moved, didn't they? They didn't destroy the place, did they? They didn't leave a lot of junk behind, did they?" She was right on all counts except for the jukebox, which I removed later. I was a charging bull when I picked up my darling at the airport, and she had reduced me to a eunuch.

I told her about the female police officer who was nice enough to give me a duplicate key to the place but she had no reaction.

I don't know why, but I started laughing. After regaining my composure, I asked my darling wife to, do me a huge favor. "Please don't rent a place to someone without talking it over with me first."

"You're right, my darling. I will never upset the apple of my eye again."

CHAPTER TWENTY-FIVE

THE SIGN CAMPAIGN

In 2002, New York City was strapped for cash. Building department foot soldiers went out on a blitzkrieg seldom seen in the history of our city to bring in the money. The statutes regarding signage had been largely ignored since the seventies. According to the law, every permanent sign owner is obligated to hire an architect to draw plans and submit them to the building department for approval. Once approved, a sign is on record and an annual filing fee is owed. The processing of these applications, because of manpower shortages and an archaic system, was never completed in a reasonable time to allow the sign owner to get signs up in a timely fashion. If a sign owner takes a chance and posts the sign before getting the permit, they risk a huge fine. The cost of processing can run into the thousands of dollars. Most storeowners are not in the Donald Trump category, so they don't have enough money or patience to put up with all the red tape. This made for the perfect climate for a successful blitzkrieg, beginning with those who failed to file.

The regular maximum penalty for noncompliance is $2,500 per sign and a minimum mitigating fine of $400 per sign, with some exceptions. There were lots of reasons for fines. For example, there was a fine for a sign not properly affixed to a surface, or when a sign was too close to another one, or partially obstructed it. They also fined you if the sign was not made within specified dimensions. To make matters worse, the bastards struck in the middle of a cold winter. One of my tenants was slammed with an exceptional $10,000 fine for only one sign. Several store owners I know personally paid the $400 minimum.

At eight-thirty on a bitterly cold and windy night, I saw with my own eyes a woman in her fifties climb a ladder with a hammer and screwdriver to jar loose a sign from the building surface. Many people replaced existing signs with cardboard. Even though cardboard signs look ugly, they're not liable for fines. Bodega owners were running to other bodega owners, warning them of impending disaster. Many closed their businesses because they couldn't afford to pay an architect. How I was affected: I owned a commercial building with seven tenants that between them posted eighteen signs. None of the tenants filed for them in the building department. A building department foot soldier found something wrong with thirteen of the signs. He then wrote a summons listing all thirteen sign violations, naming the city of New York as plaintiff and John Doe landlord as defendant. On the summons he wrote the date I had to appear in court.

They're not my signs. So why should I pay? Well, in my business, the word "fair" rarely applies. Until all the signs had been removed or brought up to code, my nervous system remained on the verge of collapse. You may be asking why I didn't demand that the prospective tenant file for his sign or signs before leasing to them. If I did that, I would have no commercial tenants.

Three of my tenants threatened to move because they couldn't afford to pay an architect and all the other assorted expenses of getting a legal sign. I went to court and paid a fine for all thirteen signs totaling $5,200. I was reimbursed $2,800 by four of my tenants. None of them, aside from the one who had been hit with the $10,000 fine, even knew they needed to file. I swallowed the $2,400 of fines that two tenants refused to pay. They were excellent tenants otherwise. Fortunately, I still had room in my esophagus for more fines to be crammed in. To this day, I firmly believe the building department planned from the beginning to fine every sign holder the mitigating amount of $400, whether or not they filled out a certificate of correction in time for the court date. I understand why in some cases owners of electric signs should be fined. An electric sign poses a potential fire hazard. Eventually, after the city felt they had extracted enough blood, they called it a day. This campaign was just another example of the dirty tricks the city employs to raise fast cash.

CHAPTER TWENTY SIX

SHORT-TERM RENTAL

ON JULY 1, 1995, I was standing near the entrance of one of my apartment buildings. Two men who looked to be from the Middle East approached me.

"Are you the owner?" one of the men asked.

"Yes," I said "What do you want to know?"

"We need one apartment for each of us. Do you have anything available now?"

They came exactly at the right time. Two apartments were empty. I asked them my usual brain-wracking questions. Both checked out. Each one gave me a month's rent and a month's security, and I let them move in right then and there. How lucky could I be?

The following day, a telephone truck pulled up to the front of the building. I walked over to the driver and asked him if he needed to go inside.

He answered my question with a question. "Are you the owner?"

"Yes," I said.

"Two of your tenants requested that we install two phone lines in each of their apartments."

"Why so many lines?"

"That's not my business, sir. If our customer wants six lines, he'll get six lines."

"I simply can't allow it" I said.

"Listen mister, I don't give two hoots in hell if you're the owner or not, go bother somebody else!"

"You're right. Install what you damn please. Do your thing and I'll leave you alone."

"Don't get your dander up, buddy; we'll be in and out of here in less than hour."

The phone guy's sidekick was standing off to the side enjoying the verbal exchange. I could tell, based on my outstanding record of judging people, that he was proud of me for putting the phone jerk in his place.

On July 14, 1995, I knocked on the second-floor tenant's door. No one was home. The third-floor tenant was also not home. I usually don't bother tenants who have just moved in until the following month's rent is due, but in this case, I was curious to see where the two phone guys had put all those jacks. I wanted to go in with my master key and look around, but I had left the keys in the car and was too lazy to go back for them.

On August 1, 1995, I once again knocked on the doors of both tenants. Neither of them was home. I returned at ten o'clock that evening, and the following morning at seven, with the same results. I smelled something fishy. Not waiting for an invitation, I took out my master key and opened the door of the second-floor apartment. The apartment was completely empty except for some dirty laundry and scattered photos in one corner of the living room. The photos showed eight young men with rifles standing in an open field. One of them was pointing his rifle at a young woman kneeling on the ground with her hands tied behind her back. I continued looking at the rest of the photos, paying attention to every detail. One of the photos interested me more than the others. It showed two soldiers also kneeling on the ground, but not tied up like the women in the other photo. This photo was not very clear, so I couldn't tell if there was somebody else in the picture besides them. Something in the next photo caught my eye. It looked like a flag, but I wasn't sure. I had already guessed that all the photos were taken somewhere in the Middle East. I was curious to find out what flag it was. My reading glasses were no help. I went downstairs to the drugstore and bought a magnifying glass. I was surprised to see it was the flag of Israel. My previous indifference suddenly changed to maximum concern. I ran up upstairs to the other apartment, anxious to learn if there were more surprises awaiting me. The upstairs apartment was also empty, except for one picture on the kitchen table showing two soldiers hugging one another, a man and a woman.

There was no reason to think that the pictures signified anything, but I kept them anyway. I put them in a folder for safe keeping. As both apartments were completely empty and free of damage, it didn't take long to get them ready for the next tenants. On August 4, I had fourteen-karat gold tenants occupying both apartments. No stories there.

Near the end of August, I noticed telephone bills piling up on the radiator of the foyer in the apartment building in question. Usually, I would throw unclaimed mail in the garbage after a week or two, but this was different. Five telephone bills were postmarked two days before, addressed to the previous tenants. I knew and still know that it's a federal crime to open someone else's mail, but I remembered the photos and felt compelled to snoop.

The first envelope held a telephone bill for $5,800. The second bill was for $3,200. The third one was for $6,800 and the last one was for $10,400. Every single call was made to a country in the Middle East, including Israel, between the 2nd and third of July. None of the calls exceeded three minutes. I felt it was my duty to notify all the agencies that I felt should know. I closed the front door so no one would see me with my mouth wide open. From the shockI began visualizing several scenarios, all of them bad. I sped home, anxious to tell my wife what I discovered. The second she opened the door to greet me,

I spurted out the whole story, starting from the first day the two men moved into their apartments, up to finding the telephone bills on the radiator. I was pretty sure they were'nt selling time slots. If they were, why did they cram it into two days? They had a whole month to do it.

She was dumbfounded. "What are you going to do, honey?"

"The first thing is to call the telephone company." I explained to the lady answering the phone the whole story. When I finished she told me that the person who handles these things is on vacation. "Is there something else I can do for you? "No," I answered. Then she asked me and I quote, "Have I provided you with outstanding service today?" Totally disgusted, I hung up the phone and called the second agency on my list, the Israeli Council. They said that it wasn't in their jurisdiction, so they couldn't help me. A big surprise, but I didn't let it deter me. Next, I called the FBI. They said that they weren't interested unless I could prove there was intent to commit a crime. I was not ready to give up, so I called the telephone company again and spoke to a different customer service representative. After she heard my story she asked me if I wanted to file a complaint? I was ready to punch her in the mouth. "Madam," does this sound like a complaint? I asked. After a second or two, a man came to the phone. "What seems to be the problem, Sir? I repeated the whole story, which was now the fifth time, if you include my wife. The man, identifying himself as the head supervisor, said that he wasn't going to pursue the matter. "We're just going to write it off,"

So that was that. My wife told me to throw all the bills into the garbage. But I couldn't. Why were all the calls made only between July 2 and July 3? They had signed one-year leases and already paid for the month of July, but barely occupied the apartments. What was the urgency? I simply couldn't understand why no one else seemed to care? I stored the bills in a secret hiding place, feeling that someday they'd prove to be important. It was strictly a feeling, nothing more.

On the morning of September 11, 2001, I had an appointment at nine o'clock with an attorney whose office was one block away from the twin towers. Just as I was getting ready to leave the house, my wife hollered something from the other room.

"Maestro, don't you remember that your accountant is calling you at nine-thirty and you have to be here to take the call?"

I had completely forgotten, and thanked her for reminding me. Forty-five minutes later, I was thanking her again. She literally saved my life. A few days later, I retrieved all the telephone bills that I had kept since 1995 and once again called the FBI. This time they were interested. They were so interested that they told me to immediately fax all the bills to their office and mail in the originals. I did what they told me to do, but never heard from them again.

CHAPTER TWENTY-SEVEN

THE ONE-FAMILY HOUSE

THE STORIES YOU'LL HEAR about this house and the tenants who occupied it may sound preposterous, but they're as true as true can be.

The sellers, Vera and Manny Wacko, were in the midst of a bitter divorce. Vera Wacko had been in and out of mental institutions for most of her adult life. Manny slept with his hooker girlfriend in the Wackos guest bedroom while Vera slept alone in the master bedroom. Their two sons were heavy into drugs, and occasionally, Manny's brother would drop in to borrow money. It's fair to call theirs a dysfunctional family. The couple was tickled pink to sell the house. The economy was bad, just like it was when I bought my first building. I had the sellers agree to be my lender, and they demanded only 5 percent down at contract. Manny drew up the contract and a mortgage payment schedule without including interest rates. The monthly payments were so low that I honestly thought he didn't know what he was doing. This deal was too good to be true. There had to be a catch. As we move along, you'll find out there was more than one.

No one told me that Mr. and Mrs. Wacko had a binding agreement that all mortgage checks be divided between them evenly. Nobody told me that the Wackos were embroiled in a war for 100 percent control of the mortgage. For the next six months, I paid them as instructed. One day, I received a legal document in the mail ordering me to pay Mrs. Wacko 100 percent of the mortgage payments going forward. My lawyer told me that she had won the fight with her husband, and I was obligated to abide by the judge's decision. I didn't hear any objections from her husband, so for the next nine months, I did as instructed. But then I received a legal notice that Mr. Wacko had won his appeal in a higher court, reversing the judge's decision in the lower court. I didn't feel like getting caught in the middle of a crossfire between opposing lawyers, so I immediately scheduled a closing to pay off the balance of my debt to Mrs. Wacko before I'd be obligated to pay her husband. The closing was going along smoothly until suddenly, Mrs. Wacko's attorney interrupted the title company rep and called me to the side.

"Mr. Carlos, I can't in good conscience let this closing go any further without revealing something to you."

"Why?" I asked.

"You promise not to tell a soul what I'm about to tell you?"

"If you say so," I responded.

"Mrs. Wacko borrowed money from an out-of-state shy lock at an exorbitant rate of interest. Your mortgage payments couldn't sustain her. The loan was never recorded and the house was used for collateral. If the loan was not recorded, there is no way anyone could know unless she told them. She told me privately that she had no intention of paying them back. You know, sir that anything discussed between a lawyer and his client must remain confidential. I'm taking a chance by telling you this. It's a breach of ethics."

"It would be a breach of ethics if you didn't tell me," I said.

The lawyer continued. "The title company is not to blame. How could they or anyone else, know about the loan if it was never recorded? The Shylock has a binding contract with Mrs.

Wacko, so unless the loan is paid in full, or you assume her debt, the house could go to foreclose. Her husband would be in the same boat as you." He was right. this Shylock company could legally take the house out from under me unless I continued to pay them instead of the Wacko bitch, or as an alternative, pay them off in entirety. i chose the late option, even though it was a lot more money than i had to pay Mrs. Wacko.

"How wonderful," I said. "I only have to pay them 50 percent of her balance at 26 percent interest. This translates to a hell of a lot of money."

But he was right. I shouldn't have complained.

I paid off the Shylock the following week, finally gaining free and clear title to the property. A purchase that I had thought was a super deal turned out to be highway robbery. I won't talk about dollars and cents. It's too painful. After the closing, I went straight home. In the mail on the floor, I saw an envelope addressed to me. It was a certified letter from the lawyer representing Mr. Wacko. In lay terms, the letter was informing me that Mr. Wacko had won the appeal and that all future mortgage payments were to be made to Mr. Wacko. I shaped the letter into an airplane and sailed it across the room. Believe it or not, it dropped straight into the garbage can. *You can whistle 'Dixie,' Wacko boy; you ain't getting a dime outta me.* Paying off Mrs. Wacko and then the shylock had drained my resources, so I was forced to take a hefty equity loan from the bank. The market was weak, so if I sold the house, I'd practically be giving it away. There was only one thing to do: Rent it to someone until the market improved. I could pay the mortgage and not lose the house in a foreclosure that way. The following tales illustrate the consequences of this decision.

PART 1: THE DENTIST

MY FIRST TENANT WAS a Dr. Gulbilly, a part-time dentist from a small town in New Jersey. He had designs of elevating his two sons and three nephews to the top of the music world. The boys had formed a band, naming it "Bang Away Sixty." According to the dentist, they were good enough to be professionals. He, with my permission, soundproofed one of his rooms and let them practice to their hearts' content.

Of course, I checked them out thoroughly before letting them move in. Of course I did. The doctor showed me tax returns, a driver's license, and references. It all met with my approval, and I didn't anticipate any problems. After all, what harm could five young musicians cause playing instruments and banging their drums in a soundproofed room? No harm, of course.

The dentist walked the streets of Manhattan daily, greasing people right and left, attempting to find someone willing to give his band an audience. Finally, he hit pay dirt. Three different moguls in the music industry agreed to hear them play. Unfortunately, all three gave thumbs down. The dentist started falling behind on his rent, stubbornly refusing to accept the fact his dream would stay a dream. The kids continued playing, at my expense of course, so I was forced to serve the dentist with a thirty-day nonpayment notice.

What a pity I didn't know that my disillusioned tenant had lost a sexual harassment lawsuit six months before we both signed the lease. But that would mean that I had conducted a thorough and comprehensive interview, and we wouldn't want that, would we? Another week passed and the five wannabes left, taking their instruments with them. At least I had inherited a soundproof room. Dr Gulbilly disappeared from the face of the earth, sticking me with four months of lost rent. But I learned a lesson from all this: no more dentists and no more bands, including orchestras. They say that from every bad experience you learn not to make the same mistake twice. That might apply to others, but not to me.

We were finished with the dentist, and I was free to put the episode behind me and move on, or so I thought. A week later, a real estate broker hired by the dentist came out from under a rocks and sued me for his commission. I never knew that deceiving bastard had even used a broker. My lawyer had asked Gullibill when we signed the lease whether he came via a broker. He had said no. I had never met this broker or had any knowledge of his existence. What was I supposed to do? How did I know the dentist was a liar? If I was so stupid as not to make sure that my lawyer inserted a clause in the lease stating that I was not responsible for broker's fees, I deserve to pay the piper. A hearing was set for the following week. There would be no jury.

Mike Mayget, the broker, and his lawyer, Vinny Stikim sat in the front row. The dentist never showed up. I came without my lawyer. Judge Bounded didn't waste any time.

"Mr. Carlos," he began, "do you know Mr. Mayget, or anyone else in his office?"

"No, your honor," I answered.

The judge turned to Mr. Mayget. "Sir, have you ever met Mr. Carlos, the defendant?"

"Yes," he answered. "He was in my office together with Dr. Gulbilly."

"It appears that someone is lying," the judge sagely observed. After scratching his forehead for a couple minutes, he turned to me. "I am sorry, Mr. Carlos, but I must rule in favor of the plaintiff."

"That's not fair, your honor," I said. "This man is an out-and-out liar. I never met this man before or heard his name mentioned."

"You may be telling the truth, sir," the judge said, "but the law, at least regarding real estate contracts with brokers, is quite clear. If there is nothing in writing to substantiate a claim, a verbal agreement is legally acceptable. As you have no one to support your testimony, I have no choice but to rule against you."

I wanted to kill the dentist, his broker, and my lawyer; all at the same time, but what I should have done first was shoot myself for being so careless. Live and learn, I guess. I wonder when that's going to happen. A week later, I had my second tenant.

PART II: MR. FRAWDER

MR. FRAWDER WAS A meticulously groomed gentleman. When I first met him, he was wearing a designer suit and a pair of expensive alligator-skin shoes. He claimed to be in the import-export business, with his main office in Cali, Colombia. You're probably wondering how I even knew he was wearing a designer suit, since I'm always running around in cheap sport jackets. The answer is simple. I asked him. He claimed his business had a branch office in Manhattan.

When I inquired what he was importing and exporting, he answered "a wide variety of paraphernalia."

"What does that include?" I asked.

"There is such a wide variety of things," he said, "I'd need two sheets of legal paper to list them all."

We both laughed. But I wish I had pressed him for more detail. Couldn't I have demanded that he be more specific? I asked him my usual probing questions that always led me directly to the essence of a potential lessee's soul. For example: *What's your name? Why do you want to rent my house, not something in Manhattan? How long have you been in business? Will you live here with someone? Can you supply me with references?* Last, but not least, *can you give me the telephone number and addresses of your Manhattan office?* Obviously, there was nothing more to learn, other than asking him for his mother's maiden name and whether or not his family arrived here on the *Mayflower*. I called his Manhattan office and spoke to his secretary. She said that their business had doubled in volume over the past year and shipping orders were piling up on her desk. After digesting all this information, I convinced myself that Mr. Frawder was okay. I took his first month's rent and another month's security, letting him move in the following day.

His next rent payment was due the first day of the following month. At five o'clock p.m. on the due date, I rang his doorbell to collect. A young Spanish man in his early twenties wearing a leather jacket opened the door to greet me. Two young girls, also wearing leather jackets, were standing behind him. Something smelled fishy but I wasn't ready to jump to conclusions. The young lad told me he was Mr. Frawder's brother and that the girls were their cousins. Seeing as none of them were on the lease, I asked him why they were here instead of Mr. Frawder. He said that his brother was in Europe buying some goods and would return in two months. I wasn't thrilled to hear this but kept quiet. My nose still told me something wasn't kosher, but I had no proof.

They paid the rent promptly on the first of the month, all in cash, even though I had told them to pay by check. When I came for my rent the following month, only the two girls were present. Once again, I could only form suspicions, nothing more. I asked them if Mr. Frawder had returned, and where their cousin was. The girls said that their cousin would be back in a few days and Mr. Frawder was still away on business, but would return next month. Again they paid in cash, even after I requested for a second time that they pay by check. On the way to my car, I noticed that the garage door was open and two motorcycles were inside. My first instinct was that two of the three residents preferred motorcycles to cars. I continued feeling that something was just not right. So instead of waiting until the first of the following month to go for the rent, I decided to pay them a surprise visit later that same month.

It was ten o'clock on a beautiful summer night, one week before the rent was due. I parked my car a block away and snuck up to the house on foot. Just as I reached the front lawn, I saw two girls hopping on motorcycles with small packages in their hands. They tied the packages with rope to the rear of their bikes and sped off into the night. The young lad, unaware that I had seen anything, opened the door to greet me. He was in pajamas and half-asleep, and asked me what I wanted at such a late hour. I made up a lie, telling him that one of his neighbors had called me, complaining about excessive noise.

"Whoever called you was mistaken," he said.

I apologized for the intrusion and returned to my car. I couldn't get the motorcycles and packages out of my mind, even though riding a motorcycle and carrying a couple of packages is nothing unusual. On the first of the following month, I again went for the rent. This time nobody was home. The motorcycles were gone and the lights were on throughout the house. I rang the doorbell but no one responded. The door was locked, so I went around to the back and peered into one of the windows, looking for a sign of life. When I was certain the house was empty, I opened the back door with my master key and went inside. Some of the furnishings I had seen on previous visits, including area rugs and blinds, were gone. In the kitchen, someone had emptied all the drawers. There was only a bottle of soda in the refrigerator. As I walked through the rest of the house, I saw that all the closets were empty. It was obvious to me that no one would return.

Later, while supervising the cleanup men, I watched the crew remove a small rug from one of the bedroom closets. I was surprised to see underneath a hole roughly three inches square carved out of the cement floor. I rolled up my sleeves and ran my hand around the bottom of the hole. It was empty. I asked myself what possible reason they had had to do such a thing. Were they nuts? Couldn't they keep their money or secret items in a bank deposit box? Oh well. I didn't have it so bad. They had been up to date on the rent and I had their security deposit.

Once again, I placed an ad in the paper for a new tenant. But this time, to gain more exposure, I gave four brokers in the area the open listing. One day, while I was dining with a friend of mine from Colombia I casually brought up the subject of Mr. Frawder and his alleged family members, just thinking it might be an interesting story for someone from the same country.

When I finished telling my friend about the hole, he looked me in the eyes and started smiling. "My dear friend," he said, "they didn't keep money in there. You missed the target. Your two girls with the bikes were probably runners transporting drugs, and the young man was most likely the dispatcher. The hole in the floor was their stash spot. It's possible they felt the law was on to them, or a competitive group was hot on their trail."

How could I have been so stupid as not to figure that out by myself? This experience taught me that if you don't do a super-duper background check, you eat crow every time. Just for the hell of it, I called Mr. Frawder's import-export company, and was not surprised to find the phone number had been disconnected. Time for another new tenant.

PART III: DR. DAPPERMIN.

A REPUTABLE BROKER THAT I had worked with in the past said that he had a solid tenant for me. The potential tenant had seen my for rent sign on the house and liked the area. He was a successful pediatrician from Argentina and, according to the broker, doing very well for himself. Did I finally have a winner?

His wife showed up alone for the question-and-answer session. She told me that her husband, Dr. Dappermin, was sick and tired of paying so much for taxes and malpractice insurance in Argentina, and had convinced her to come to America with him. I asked her why they hadn't come together to meet with me.

"He is too busy finishing last-minute odds and ends. Besides, we have similar tastes, so he trusts me to find suitable living accommodations. I'm sure if you rent your house to me he'll have no objections."

"In America," I said, "he'll also have to pay high taxes and a lot of money for malpractice insurance. Usually, both husband and wife must work to make ends meet."

She was all ears.

I continued my questioning: "What is your husband's specialty? How long has he been in practice? Is his record clean?"

"Absolutely," she said.

I should have called Argentina's health board for confirmation, but was too lazy. Besides, my nose told me she was okay. The only problem was that my nose was stuffed. Dappermin's wife paid me the first month's rent and two months security and I gave her the key. On rent day on the first of the following month, a young man dressed in a beautiful silk robe with a silk scarf wrapped around his neck answered the door and invited me in. The house was now filled with artifacts and expensive-looking trinkets. I noticed an expensive-looking Persian carpet in the living room. I also saw a brand-new billiards table, complete with brand-new sticks in a wall rack, and a colorful tapestry affixed to the living room wall.

The tenants had hired a landscaper to level the backyard's terrain and plant bushes. All these improvements were wonderful, but they triggered my suspicion. How could a young pediatrician, complaining about high expenses in a much cheaper country, afford to spend that kind of money?

I asked him as much directly. "Doctor Dappermin, are you sure you'll be able to pay $3,500 in rent?"

"Watch me" was his response.

The broker who had brought them to me knew the doctor's first cousins, who lived somewhere in Queens. This helped to assuage my fear that Dappermin was a phony and possibly engaged in something other than medicine. I could always check with the cousins to back up his story. But on the other hand, who knows if the cousins knew Dappermin well enough to vouch for him? I decided to close my eyes and pray that everything would be okay. I couldn't be unlucky all the time.

On rent day the following month, Dr. Dappermin invited me in to meet his six-year-old son. On the way to the playroom, he showed me a beautiful chandelier that he had recently installed in the dining room. He'd done so much home improvement that the house's value had almost certainly gone up. What a bonus! He always paid me in cash. I remember asking him in the beginning why he didn't pay in checks. He told me he hadn't had time to open an American bank account, but he would in the next few days. His hand would go into his pocket and pull out a wad of money. Then, with lightning speed, like you see crack dealers do in the movies, he'd count out thirty-five $100 bills and put them in my hands. Boy, this was one cool cat!

One night three weeks into the following month, I got a call from a friend of mine living two blocks away from Dappermin. My friend said that for the past two days, at about three in the morning, he had seen all the lights on at Dappermin's house. I didn't wait for an invitation; I immediately drove over. I looked through the large bay window on the front porch but didn't see anyone inside. I rang the bell, but no one answered. The door was locked. I snuck around to the back of the house. That door was also closed but not locked. I went inside, and after looking around, was pretty sure that no one was ever coming back. In one of the bedrooms, much to my surprise, I saw dirty underwear scattered over the entire floor. All the dresser drawers were empty. In the den, I saw three or four pool sticks and the doctor's robe on top of the pool table. The rancid odor from the rotten food in the fridge made me hold my nose. There were dirty dishes stacked up in the sink drawing flies, and in the child's bedroom, dirty laundry was piled half way to the ceiling.

The following day, I called the broker for some answers. She told me that the Dappermins probably had an emergency come up back in Argentina and had stored their belongings in a warehouse for a while until things got back to normal.

"I'm sure they'll return soon," she said.

I didn't believe her and let her know why.

But all was not lost. I had their security deposit and enough time to find a new tenant.

As far as I was concerned, the broker was out of the picture. I took the liberty of confiscating the pool table, the chandelier, and anything else that struck my fancy. The broker warned me not to, but after I had reminded her how her clients had screwed me, she backed off. It took me four days to clean the house to my satisfaction. A few days later, while sipping my morning coffee, I noticed a small article on an inside page of the newspaper, describing how three people in Queens had been murdered in their sleep. I wouldn't have paid much attention to it if the broker hadn't told me that the doctor had cousins living in that area. After reading the article, I put the newspaper aside and finished my breakfast. Ten minute later, the phone rang. It was the broker.

"Mr. Carlos, you have to stay away from the house. Mr. Dappermin's cousins were murdered in their sleep, and someone may come to the house looking for him. God forbid you get caught in the middle."

"What the fuck did you get me involved in, lady?" I shouted. Then, after a minute or two i calmed down and apologized for my outburst. I was too damn angry to thank her for the warning. That was the last time I ever heard from her. I'm sure the doctor, or whatever he was, knew that he was also a target. That's most likely the reason he left without saying good-bye. I stayed away from the house for a week, until I thought it was safe to go back and finish cleaning. When all the odds and ends were taken care of, I put an ad in the *Times* seeking a new tenant. I'm beginning to sound like a broken record. But I learned something: I ought to interview brokers as well as tenants, and enlist Interpol plus the CIA to help with background checks.

PART IV: THE ABADABOOS

My next tenants were a sweet, harmless-looking family from Iran. They had left their country shortly after the shah was deposed, just before Khomeini took over. They were all living in a five-bedroom apartment near the house. They were reluctant to stay in their apartment because the landlord was selling the building and might kick them out.

The family consisted of Mr. and Mrs. Abadaboo, their two sons, Abdul and Abood, and two elderly ladies from Azazel or some place sounding like that. Actually, who cares where they came from? Both sons had designs of becoming rich in a very short time. None of the six people spoke English very well, so I had an Iranian acquaintance of mine interview them on my behalf. Maybe that was a good thing. Usually, when I conducted interviews, I'd wind up sinking in a heap of horse manure. Mr. Abadaboo and his wife worked in a textile mill. Their pay stubs showed that they could afford the rent. The sons were in their early twenties, still looking for an empty lot in the Bronx to sell used cars from. While waiting for that lot, they sold used cars on the street in a busy area of Brooklyn. The first two or three months of their lease passed without incident.

One day, while driving past the house, I saw at least seven cars parked in the driveway and two or three cars in the street near the house. This wasn't unusual. Most Iranian families are large. When I drove by the following weekend, there was an added twist. The Abadaboo boys were selling cars from the driveway. In a residential area, this is a no-no. I pulled over to the curb, calling Abood over to my car.

"Mr. Abood," I said, "you are not allowed to sell cars from my property or from any other property classified as residential. That's the law."

He apologized, telling me that he understood and would stop immediately.

The following day I got a letter from the local building department, warning me that if I continued selling cars from my driveway, I would be subject to a $5,000 fine. The local village gave me three days to comply. The letter also warned that if I chose to ignore the warning, all cars parked in the driveway would be impounded, and the fine would go up to $10,000. Needless to say, I drove over in a flash. I saw four cars parked on the driveway, but neither son was there. Things were getting out of hand. I had to find these punks and find them fast. The two elderly ladies from Azazel—I like to refer to them as the Dumadum sisters—were the only ones in the house, but were useless. Either they didn't understand what I asked them, or didn't want to tell me anything. Adding to my frustration, they tried shoving tea down my throat. I needed tea like I needed a hole in my head. The only thing left to do was to wait for the two sons to return.

But then I thought for a minute. If my previous demands to stop selling cars had been ignored, why should they listen to me now? Instead of confronting them alone, I called a cop that I knew from the local precinct, explaining the whole story about the cars. He gladly agreed to help. The tactic worked. The minute the Abadaboo brothers saw the officer, they began shaking. The officer hardly had to say a word. Just his ominous look was enough inducement for them to act. Two days later, just before the village was about ready to clamp down on me, the cars disappeared. I was both happy and worried. I was happy the cars were gone, but worried that it if the brothers didn't find a commercial spot to sell them, I'd have to depend solely on their parents to pay the rent. I preferred a little cushion.

One month later, while I was collecting the rent from Mrs. Abadaboo, she asked me if it was okay to put a few goats in the backyard.

I laughed. "Of course you can," I said. "And, if you want, you can also put a couple of elephants back there."

I was joking. She wasn't. A week later, I saw one of the Dumadum sisters leading a goat from the front yard to the backyard. I followed her and was surprised to find two wooden shacks filled with hay. The stench was unbearable. A goat was inside one shack and another goat was roaming around the yard.

I threw up my hands. The cars were better than goats.

One of the sisters noticed my anger. "Mrs. Abadaboo told me that you and your wife gave us permission to have the goats. Why are you so mad-looking?"

"You're right," I said. "But I never thought you were serious."

"Well, you should have known," she said.

Oh boy, had I walked into it. Trouble was just around the corner. It didn't take long for my prediction to come true. The next day, two visitors from the village were at my doorstep. The men told me that the entire neighborhood was holding their noses and that if I didn't get rid of the goats in two days, I'd be subject to fines from the building department, health department, and the local village. They warned me that the accumulated fines could run close to $20,000.

One of the visitors really hammered the situation home. "The judge may decide to slap you harder. Remember, you are a two-time offender and a menace to the community."

My adorable tenants played dumb. They weren't about to remove the goats. I was the one under the gun, not them. If I didn't act fast, the goats would establish permanent residency and I'd have to file an application for a green card on their behalf. I needed a plan. I was not going to depend on anyone but myself to get rid of the goats. I knew a guy from way back who was something of a fixer—his name was Pullit. I offered him and a buddy of his $200 each to disappear the miserable, pain-in-the-ass goats. Pullit and his pal Yankaway didn't hesitate to say yes.

We launched our mission at three in the morning. Everyone in the house was asleep, I hoped. Three goat thieves were ready to commit the greatest theft in the annals of crime history. Under the cover of darkness, we all tiptoed our way to the backyard. Luckily, there wasn't a full moon. When the goats first saw us, they began neighing or whatever the hell it is they do, but not loud enough for anyone else to hear. So far, the heist was going a lot easier than I had expected. Pullit lassoed one goat around the neck with a heavy rope, and gently led it inside their truck. Yankaway followed suit with the other goat.

Let's review my accomplishments. I had already established myself as a professional car thief, suspected procurer, rat killer, and falsifier of a certificate of correction. I could add goat thief to the list. I paid Yankaway and Pullit their money, instructing them where to dump the goats and emphasizing that they should not harm them. I could live with the reputation of a rat killer, but not a goat killer. This had to be the perfect crime. There could be no mistakes or witnesses. When Yankaway phoned me that the goats were comfortably settled in their new environment, I breathed a sigh of relief. The village was so ecstatic that the goats had moved from the neighborhood that they gave me additional time to dismantle the shacks, throw away the hay, and clean up the yard.

The Abadaboos never said a word to anyone about the goats disappearing. They knew the entire neighborhood hated residential goats. Soon afterward, the Abadaboos stopped paying rent. I learned that Abood and his brother Abdul had finally succeeded in renting a car lot, but couldn't sell any cars. Also, Mr. and Mrs. Abadaboo were laid off from their jobs at the textile mill. That was all I needed, six deadbeats living in my house for free. I wanted to throw all of them out, but there are laws in this country. The only way I could get rid of them was to start a nonpayment action.

During their tenancy, the Abadaboos had become friendly with Mr. and Mrs. Mashuga; a married couple living across the street. The husband was a lawyer who once tried renting garage space from me. I had refused, explaining to him that I sometimes parked there and that my wife had just purchased a new car that we didn't have enough room for in my garage at home. I remembered his nasty reaction. During the second week of litigation, the Abadaboos fired their lawyer and hired Mr. Mashuga to replace him. The case dragged on for a month until the Abadaboos's stall tactics ran their course and an eviction date was set on the calendar. I knew that even though I had succeeded in getting a money judgment, I'd never see any money. At least they were going to have to vacate. The marshal was scheduled to come in twenty-three days. I was drooling in anticipation.

On the eviction day, the marshal was there along with the movers. Four of the tenants were sitting on the front lawn. The other two, the two biddies, were sitting on bridge chairs darning socks with stoic expressions on their faces. It was almost humorous watching them. The movers were making significant progress until suddenly I saw Mr. Mashuga running like crazy toward the house. The wily bastard had succeeded in getting a temporary stay from some moron judge who probably signed the document without reading it. Mashuga was trying to prevent the movers from taking any more things out of the house. The law states that if the movers had taken less than half the evicted party's belongings out, the marshal would be obligated to stop them and let them move back into the house. If this happened, I'd have to put up with them for at least another month. Thankfully the marshal determined that more than half of the house's contents were already removed. What criteria did he use? How the hell do I know? I took great pleasure watching that son of a bitch lawyer pout and sulk like a child when he realized that he was too late.

This miserable experience cost me $800 for the marshal, $1,700 for the movers, $3,500 for the lawyer, $1,500 for the cleanup crew and $15,000 in loss of rent, which I partially recovered. You're probably wondering how the Abadaboos could afford paying Mashuga for his services. They all dragged out of the house their beautiful carpet, which weighed a ton, and spread it on the grass. Mashuga, along with two other men living in the neighborhood, dragged it all the way to his driveway across the street. Mashuga was huffing and puffing so much I thought he'd drop dead before reaching his destination. The following week, to show my appreciation to the lord above, I helped an old man cross the street. The day after, I accompanied an old man who was limping on his way to the super market. The following Saturday, I prayed to the mighty one above for all the wrong reasons. I prayed that he'd find me a good tenant.

PART V: THE COBRAS

MR. AND MRS. COBRA and their eight-year-old son came through a broker who had a solid reputation. They were the last tenants to live in the house. You could not ask for a more charming couple. Mr. Cobra was an electrician and his wife was a neophyte lawyer, just starting to practice.

Finally, I had found tenants with class and integrity. People who paid by check, not cash. People who kept their apartment clean so I wouldn't have to call an exterminator every other day. People who drove cars, not motorcycles. People who didn't curse in every other other sentence. People, if they are guilty, pay an ECB violation and people who have a high credit rating. To celebrate my good fortune, I went to the nearest bar and got drunk as a skunk, postponing the interview one day until I could sober up.

As I had failed myself as an interrogator of potential tenants, I decided to bring my wife with me for the interview. I began my questioning. My wife stood by, listening intently. Seeing as she didn't interrupt me, I felt I was asking the right questions. But just before I asked the next one, my wife whispered something in my ear.

"This bitch will only step into this house over my dead body. There's no way in hell I'll let her in here. Trust me, dear. I have good sense. I know what I'm talking about."

"My dear," I said, "don't be ridiculous. Mr. Cobra makes the decisions. Didn't you see that he was answering the questions, not her? Also, didn't you see how she obeyed him when he told her, not asked her, to bring his jacket from the car? She only said one thing throughout the interview. How could you be so tough on her?"

"One thing is all I need to hear," my wife replied. "You'll see that I'm right."

I couldn't see how my wife could have found anything to object to in Mrs. Cobra. Mr. Cobra was the man, and Mrs. Cobra was the mouse. Case closed. Their lease contained a clause that the Cobras had the option to buy the house at a later date. The price would be based on the finding of two independent appraisers. My wife continued pouting, and when I couldn't take it any more, I told her to go home and let me deal with them alone. For the next four months, everything was peachy-creamy.

But one morning, the phone rang.

"It's for you, darling. It's our tenant, Mrs. Cobra." She was calling for my wife.

After a few minutes of talking, my wife turned red. "No, definitely not. I will not allow you to change any tiles in the kitchen or any other room in the house. If you buy the house, you can do what you want." My wife grabbed my arm as soon as she hung up the phone. "Mr. Know-it-all, you are coming with me to confront that bitch. I'm not going there alone."

While driving there, I started thinking about what size dress would be appropriate for me. Macy's had a sale on.

The minute we got to the house my wife went after Mrs. Cobra. "I do not allow you to make any changes or alterations of any kind without my permission. Is that clear?"

Mrs. Cobra barked right back. "Madam, I am paying top rent. So if I see that your kitchen and bathroom tiles are ugly, I'm going to change them, with or without your permission."

My wife grabbed a broom and was ready to strike Mrs. Cobra, but I yanked it away from her in the nick of time. Two women duking it out was the last thing I needed. It was time to reassert my manhood. I told my wife in a firm tone of voice to stand back and let me handle things. It's a shame that Mr. Cobra wasn't around. He would have straightened his wife out immediately. But Mr. Cobra was not there, so I had to take his place.

I addressed Mrs. Cobra. "Maybe we can defuse this thing and reach a compromise. Instead of replacing the kitchen tiles with dark beige, would a lighter shade be acceptable to you?"

"That depends," she said. "I'd have to see the color before committing myself."

Suddenly, Mrs. Cobra was telling me what to do with my own property. Was there a possibility that my wife had been right about this woman? Nah, I simply had to find her husband. I convinced my wife and Mrs. Cobra to go together and chose tiles that would be suitable to both of them. Just to play it safe, I joined them in case a fistfight would break out. They visited four stores before finally finding the right color. On the way back, Mrs. Cobra told my wife that we would have to pay the labor costs for inserting the tiles, because, she said, the new tiles added value to the house. My wife looked like she was ready to smack her in the face, but restrained herself. She told her that she'd been overly co-operative with her but there was no way in hell she'd pay for installing the tiles.

Surprisingly, Mrs. Cobra backed off.

At dinner, I tried telling my wife that one swallow doesn't make a drink, but she was in no mood to listen. When we finished eating, she suggested that we go to the house to see if the tiles had been installed properly. My wife was very happy with what she saw and complimented Mrs. Cobra for choosing the right person to do the job. Could it be that the two of them would now start loving one another? It seemed possible. It's also possible that, at any moment, the ceiling would fall on my head. My wife then asked Mrs. Cobra's permission to tour the house to see what improvements had she made.

"Come and see for yourself," Mrs. Cobra said. My wife and I joined her in Mrs. Cobra's son's bedroom. On the mantel were several artifacts from different parts of the globe. We both complimented her on her choice of wallpaper. I was ecstatic how a hostile climate had quickly changed to a friendly one. It was the perfect time to invite the Cobras to our home for dinner, maybe even time to buy four tickets to a Broadway show. But in a split second, a beautiful scenario turned into a catastrophe.

When the three of us entered the master bedroom, my wife noticed that the Cobras had replaced the beautiful, expensive drapes that my wife had left with cheap and ugly ones. To add fuel to the fire, my wife noticed that in one corner of the room, her drapes were squeezed into a box along with other miscellaneous junk.

"Who gave you the right to throw my drapes in the garbage?" she asked. "You're going to remove them from the box, iron them, and put them right back where you found them."

For the first time, Mrs. Cobra showed her real self. "Fuck you," she said.

"Fuck me?" My wife answered back. "I guess you can't be civilized, so why should I be?" My wife grabbed Mrs. Cobra around the neck and threw her against the wall. Mrs. Cobra bounced off the wall like a rubber ball and landed in a swivel chair that spun her around in a circle three or four times. She remained in the chair for a full minute, in total shock. It was high time for me to get the hell out of there. I grabbed my wife by the arm and rapidly ushered her to my car. She cursed me out all the way home, using words that you can't find in the dictionary. I felt like a jerk for not listening to her from the start. But perhaps Mr. Cobra would show up and save the day. I got a hold of him and asked what we should do about the drape issue.

His response: "I have no time to get involved. Do whatever you want. I could care less."

It was time for me to take charge and deal with Mrs. Cobra. I let things simmer down for a day or two and then called her, saying that I wanted to see her alone, promising that I wouldn't bring my wife with me. I made it clear to my wife that from now on, she had to stay out of the picture with the Cobras. She was too emotionally drained to argue. Mrs. Cobra agreed to meet me in two hours. I told her that I had reached the end of my patience and if she raised her voice to me like she did with my wife, she'd be sorry.

She greeted me at the door and before I said a word she said, Mr. Carlos, I beg of you not to hurt me," I sensed the trepidation in her voice.

"Of course not," I said. "I merely want to talk to you like a human being and try to improve the atmosphere." I promised her that my wife would no longer bother her. I told her that the matter of the drapes had been blown out of proportion. "The truth is, Mrs. Cobra, "I didn't like the drapes any more than you did."

She smiled and gave me a light kiss on the cheek. "It's so nice to talk to someone that listens to reason," she said. "Why can't your wife be like you?"

"I don't know. But it doesn't matter any more. If you want to talk about anything at all, you talk only to me, okay?"

"Thank you, Mr. Carlos. I sure feel better now."

For a while, things were quiet. I didn't hear a word from either one of the Cobras. We had reached the fourteenth month of their tenancy, with ten months to go before they could, once a price was agreed upon, exercise their option to buy.

One morning, my wife handed me the phone. "Someone wants to speak to you dear," she said.

It was Mrs. Cobra. I took the phone to another room and listened to what she had to say.

"Could you come over by yourself? There's something I'd like to discuss with you."

"I'd be happy to," I said. "We haven't heard from you for a while. I hope everything is all right." I thought about telling my wife about the conversation, but didn't see a need at the time.

Mrs. Cobra cordially greeted me at the door and invited me in. After we finished with the small talk, she came to the point. "Remember, Mr. Carlos, we all agreed that we have the option to buy the house when the lease expires?"

"Yes," I answered. "So what are you saying?"

"My husband and I want to exercise our option to purchase your house now instead of waiting until the lease expires."

"I don't see any problem with that," I said. "But you remember how we agreed to establish the price?"

"Yes, she answered. You and I have to hire independent appraisers to determine the market value."

"But you should know as well as I do, your appraiser may be slightly on the low side and mine may be slightly on the high side. Therefore, we'll probably have to compromise on the price."

She nodded her understanding.

I asked where her husband was. She told me he was at work.

At dinner, I informed my wife about my meeting with Mrs. Cobra, only because her signature was on the lease, giving her the right to know about a potential sale.

"I'm happy you didn't tell me," she said. "I don't want to see her face. Just pay me the courtesy of letting me know when you agree on the price. I don't have to be at the closing. I can't stand that woman. If she tries stealing the house, you damn well better tell that bitch to go back to hell where she came from."

The appraisers quickly reached their respective conclusions. My appraiser did a thorough job, comparing the property to similar houses in the area to provide market context. My wife and I were satisfied with his results. The Cobras' appraiser determined that our house was worth about $200,000 less than we thought. I was positive the Cobra's hired an appraiser to do what they told him to do. Several houses in the area, comparable to mine, had recently sold for at least $200,000 more than he said our house was worth.

I was angry and shocked, and had no idea what criteria he had used. Unless I could prove that their appraiser was a phony, I'd have to live with the results.

My wife had to know. "You idiot," she screamed. "Why didn't you listen to me in the beginning? Look what you caused."

I waited a couple of days until things simmered down and then called Mrs. Cobra. "Mrs. Cobra, can I come over? Maybe you and I can work this thing out. C'mon," I gingerly pleaded, "we've solved impasses before."

"Okay," she said, "but please don't come with your wife."

I promised her that I wouldn't. On this visit, Mrs. Cobra was not very nice. After some sharp words were exchanged, my man, Mr. Cobra entered the room. At last! My troubles were over. I could dream, couldn't I? It's like the fellow who keeps putting money in the jukebox figuring that, eventually, he'd hear the song. We shook hands and he retreated to the other room.

"Get your ass back here, mister," his wife shouted. "You're part of this. Just keep your mouth shut. I'll do all the talking."

I hated to admit it, but my wife had been right. Mr. Cobra was strictly window dressing.

I needed to get tough again. "Madam," I said. "I'm done kissing your backside. You'll do what I say or move out. I'm giving you an option. You can take it or leave it. Your so-called appraiser said my house is worth $250,000. Is that right? That's at least $200,000 less than it is worth. You want the house? You pay me $475,000. If not, keep your bazoo shut and continue paying me my rent. Don't worry! I won't sue you for breaking the lease."

Mrs. Cobra appeared to be in total shock. Mr. Cobra, who I'll now refer to as the tree stump, remained mute. I thought that maybe Mrs. Cobra had seen that she couldn't have it her way any more. I was dead wrong. Instead of taking a step back, she took two steps forward.

"You sons of bitches, you want to play games with me? I'll show you a thing or two. You'll pay dearly for this. Just wait and see. Now get the hell out of my house."

As I left, I thought I saw a piece of bark peeling off the tree stump but I probably was imagining it. I didn't understand at the time what paying dearly meant. If I had known, the gruesome events that followed might never have taken place.

It didn't take long for Mrs. Cobra to exact her revenge. First, she stopped paying rent. There were only six months left on the lease, so she would probably get away with it. After giving them some extra time to see if she was bluffing, I found a lawyer to start a nonpayment action.

CHAPTER TWENTY-EIGHT

THE NON-PAYMENT ACTION

WILLY GETTEM, MY LATEST lawyer, was a giant of a man, wearing size sixteen shoes and specially tailored extra-large suits from Hong Kong. He shook my hand, but before he could squeeze my knuckles to death, I quickly withdrew my hand. I had been lucky with Longalux and was not ready to push my luck with Gettem.

"I don't see anything so complicated here, Mr. Carlos. We'll serve your tenant with a thirty-day notice and if they fail to respond, we'll go straight to a holdover. If they don't pay, they'll be out of your house in a maximum of sixty days."

On the twenty-ninth day of the thirty-day notice, Mr. Stikkem, partner in the firm, Stikkem, Slappem, and Smakkem, representing the Cobras, called Willy and asked him to allow his clients two more weeks to come up with the money. Willy knew that any judge would grant Stikkem his wish so he kept quiet. Two weeks passed and, once again, Stikkem told my lawyer that his clients needed a little more time because their private lender was still out of town. The court date was pushed back seventeen days.

By the time the court date came, Judge Seegood was in no mood to play games. "Mr. Stikkem," he said, "I've given you enough leeway. It's time to move on."

Just as Willy was about to speak, Mrs. Cobra shouted for all to hear. "Your honor, Mr. Carlos did not sign the thirty day notice. The signature there is not his. It's clear to me that someone else signed his name."

I stretched open my mouth in disbelief.

"Mr. Stikkem, are you aware of this?" asked the judge.

"No, your honor, my client never told me. This is the first time I've heard it," Stikkem said.

"Mr. Gettem, do you have anything to say?" the judge asked.

"Definitely, your honor. This is just another maneuver by my adversary to buy time for his clients, and I hope you can see through it, your honor."

"Mr. Stikkem, do you have proof that your client's claim is justified?"

"I'll know as soon as you do your honor."

Mrs. Cobra handed her attorney a letter that I had written to her in an attempt to smooth things out after all the fighting with my wife. She showed Mr. Stikkem that my signature at the end of the letter did not match my signature on the thirty-day notice. The judge, growing impatient, asked Mr. Stikkem to bring the letter and the thirty-day notice to the bench. I remember holding my breath and praying the judge would dismiss the ploy. Two or three agonizing minutes passed and the suspense was over.

"I'm sorry, people," the judge said. "I can't, in good conscience, say unequivocally that the same person signed the two signatures. Mr. Gettem, I am giving you thirty days to prove to me beyond a reasonable doubt that Mr. Carlos did in fact sign the thirty-day notice. Otherwise, you will have to start the proceeding from scratch."

Needless to say, I was livid. I didn't remember ever seeing the thirty-day notice but that's not unusual with all the papers I see on a daily basis. I asked Gettem to show it to me so I could see what every one was talking about. It didn't take me a second to realize it wasn't my signature. I turned toward my lawyer.

"Mr. Gettem, you've got some explaining to do"

"I'm sorry, Mr. Carlos. I couldn't find you and it was getting too close to the deadline. I had to sign it or we would lose at least sixty days."

"Beautiful," I said. "Now how do you intend to get me out of this mess so I don't have to start the case all over and lose another ninety days?"

"I know a malleable handwriting expert, Mr. Dewover, that will train you to duplicate my handwriting," he said. "But after you pass his test, you'll have to apply for a new driver's license, new credit cards, and other forms of ID that you normally carry in your wallet."

CHAPTER TWENTY-NINE

JOHN DEWOVER

JOHN DEWOVER WAS A real pro. I could only wonder how much money he raked in teaching people a different signature than their own. One week later, I was an adept forger. Add this to my list of criminal accomplishments. Don't ask what the observant Cobra bitch cost me, both financially and emotionally.

Thirty two days later, the non payment case of Carlos against Cobra resumed

Judge Seegood began by addressing my attorney. "Mr. Gettem, did you bring me the proof I requested?"

"Yes, your honor."

"Let's see what you have, counselor."

The judge examined all the documents from my wallet, comparing them to my signature on the thirty-day notice. After three or four agonizing minutes, the judge declared his findings.

"People, I have determined that the signature on the thirty-day notice is that of Mr. Carlos. I trust, Mr. Stikkem, that this will be the final stall maneuver we'll have to put up with in this case. Now let's continue"

Stikkem didn't have much of a defense. His only recourse was to drag things out as long as possible. Forty days before the lease terminated, the trial was over. Judge Seegood ordered Mrs. Cobra to pay all back rent, and if she failed to do so, we could go straight into a holdover and arrange for the marshal to evict both her and the tree stump. I was dead certain she wouldn't pay me a dime, and even if I was lucky enough to get a money judgment against her, I'd probably wind up using it for toilet paper. My wife and I set a date with the marshal for February 16, twenty-one days before the lease expired. We stewed in our juices, waiting for the date to arrive.

It was the morning of February 13, three days before the marshal was scheduled to come. My wife and I were having breakfast when the phone rang. It was Gus, the same guy who had tipped me off on another occasion that all the lights at the Cobra property were on.

"Mr. Carlos, I think you should come over to your house as soon a possible. For the past two days, I've heard loud pounding, but the lights in the house are always off. I have a bad feeling about it."

I didn't stand on formalities. I got into my car and drove right over. It was nine degrees below zero. The wind chill factor made it feel like twenty below. There were no birds chirping. The sun was peeking out of the clouds. Newspapers were stuck to the ice in several driveways. While driving there, I imagined the worst. It wasn't long before my suspicions turned to reality. I could not believe what I found at the rental house.

CHAPTER THIRTY

MASS DESTRUCTION

THE HOUSE WAS TOTALLY dark. The front door was wide open. The second I entered the vestibule, I found myself standing in three to four inches of water. All the pipes had burst, flooding the house. I ran outside to the shack containing the boiler. Sure enough, all the connecting wires were snipped. I darted back into the house, discovering more than forty light switch covers removed and their wires exposed. Without warning, my wife collapsed on the living room carpet. I poured water on her face. She started screaming and kept it up for at least five minutes before passing out for a second time. She was having a nervous breakdown. I carried her to the car and drove straight to the nearest mental hospital. The minute I passed through the gates, the depressing scene prompted me to schedule an evaluation for myself.

A Dr. Glummer ushered my wife to a private room and told me that I could stay with her for only a few minutes. When I saw she was nonresponsive, barely listening to me, I decided to leave and check with the doctor the following day.

On the seventh day of her stay, Dr. Glummer released her into my care. As I couldn't be with her around the clock, I hired a nurse to fill in for me. I drove back to the house to see what else was damaged. Human feces were strewn over the living room carpet. All the expensive area rugs in the bedrooms and hallway were torn to shreds and reeking from mildew. The toilets were smeared with excrement. Windows throughout the house were smashed beyond repair. All the telephone lines were severed; all the kitchen cabinets slashed with a knife or other sharp instrument. All the expensive drapes we provided them, except for the ones Mrs. Cobra had hated, were removed from the premises. The garage door was destroyed, probably the work of an axe. All the ceiling fixtures in the house were missing, their wires exposed. The dishwasher was yanked from its place and smashed with a blunt object; the beautiful stove we provided smashed to smithereens. To my surprise, they never touched the refrigerator. But Mrs. Cobra had made sure to keep spoiled food inside. The floor was littered with wet newspapers and cat litter. The bedspreads stank from urine. The skylight glass in the living room was shattered. The air conditioning unit outside the house had been hammered repeatedly with a blunt instrument. The in-ground swimming pool was chipped on all four sides. This damage alone would cost me over $20,000 to repair. After all this, it's still possible that I forgot something. But does it matter? How much worse could it be? I don't feel like mulling over the possibilities.

The first thing I needed to do was suck out the water from all the carpets. This was no easy task. It took three guys with water pumps and other suction devices to get enough water out so that it would be possible to drag the carpets out of the house. Finding a place to dump them came later. There was too much water in the walls and ceilings to do any rewiring, so I had to wait a few days before calling an electrician. The next order of business was rewiring the boiler. The house needed heat. Aside from the guys who sucked out the water, there was no other worker willing to set foot in a damp, freezing house. Finding a boiler man ready to work in these conditions was not easy.

PART I: JOHN SALUSHIN

AFTER AN HOUR OF frustrating calls to boiler men, I spotted an ad in the *Penny Saver.* "Plumber needs work. Call 12345. Leave message."

I left a message. Five minutes later, the phone rang.

"This is John Salushin. What can I do for you?"

"We have a boiler that doesn't work," I said. "Could you please help us to get it started?" I didn't want to scare him away, so I avoiding talking about all the snipped wire and the fact that the boiler was in a shack outside the house.

"I'll be there in an hour," John said.

He was a man of his word. He was driving a jalopy that looked like it was ready to self-destruct at any moment. I couldn't believe that his car could hold up for ten minutes, let alone one hour, in this freezing weather.

John was a muscular man, standing six feet four inches tall. He weighed about 240 pounds and had gorilla-sized hands. I was positive that once he saw that the boiler was in a backyard shack, he'd do an about-face and return to Staten Island. I was dead wrong. John put on a pair of gloves, got on his back, and slithered his way into the shack. He told me to stay in my car and put on the heat.

"No sense two of us freeze to death," he said.

I took his advice. Two hours later, I woke up from a sound sleep. *I better see how John is doing*, I said to myself.

I couldn't believe what I saw when I went back to the shack. John was in the same position I had left him in. I could see steam exuding from his mouth.

"One more hour, Mr. Carlos, and I'll have this baby running," he said.

This was one hell of a man. My respect for him grew by the minute.

Just as he said, one hour later he had the boiler running. I'll never forget how he looked crawling out of the shack. His face was frostbitten. He could barely move his fingers, and when he tried to stand, his legs wouldn't support him, causing him to fall to the ground. With all his might, he stood up again and shook each leg for a minute or two until he regained some feeling. I thanked him several times. When he tried to respond, his lips were so frozen he could barely get the words out. He showed me a V for victory and I put seven $100 bills in his hand. I never saw or heard from John Salushin again.

PART II: THE TEN PERCENT MAN

NOW THAT THE HOUSE was warm, I invited Ken Riggit, a freelance insurance claim adjustor, referred to in the trade as a 10 percent man, to assess the damage before starting to put the house back in shape. A 10 percent man usually works out a financial agreement with the insurance company representative so all three of us—claim adjustor, property owner, and insurance company—can be reasonably satisfied. Ken and I walked together through all the rooms, and I could see that he was having difficulty believing the horrific scene before his eyes. Ken was not stupid. He knew that I wasn't the guilty one. But he also knew that my insurance company had found the Cobras and questioned them. I don't know how they did it, but the Cobras had convinced my insurance company that I had done all the damage to collect the insurance.

Why didn't my insurance company question me? I guess it was easier to believe the Cobras so that they could conveniently reject my claim and avoid paying me. I explained to Ken the whole story from the time the Cobras and I first met. I asked him, if I was trying to blame everything on the Cobras, why would I have to spend so much time methodically destroying practically every damn thing in the house? Was it necessary that I get on my hands and knees, chip away over forty tiles in the kitchen, go out to the swimming pool in freezing weather and smash tiles in it, spend time removing over forty covers from the light switch boxes and expose the wiring in every one of them?

"Doesn't it make more sense to think that Mrs. Cobra had decided that if she couldn't have the house, neither could we?" I said to Ken.

"I'm inclined to agree with you," he said. "This appears to be the work of a maniac." Ken took a jillion pictures and told me that he'd be in touch.

Three and a half months later, the house was finally in shape to rent or sell The balance of the work on the wiring and pipes was nothing compared to what John accomplished. All the money for materials and labor came out of my pocket, and we hadn't received a dime from the insurance at that point, so I had to borrow some money from a bank to stay afloat. If my wife had a gun, she probably would have used it on Mrs. Cobra, and me too, for that matter. The whole thing was simply too much for her to bear. I took her back to the hospital for the second time and she stayed there for two months until the doctors decided she was fit to be released. My own condition? Somehow, the men in white coats didn't haul me off in a straight jacket.

I didn't have a clue where the Cobras went, but the insurance company sure did. But I knew damn well they wouldn't tell me a thing; it was strictly up to me to find the Cobras. I figured that they were probably in lousy shape financially, so they'd be renting, probably not too far from their former residence, because their child was attending high school two blocks away and Mr. Cobra's business was close by. I decided to track them down using utilities records. Landlords usually have service in their name, but tenants often pay their own electric bills. That's where I would start.

PART III: THE LADY AT CON EDISON

I waited on line to speak to a customer service representative at the Con Edison Electric Company. The minute I was called,

I complimented the lady on her looks, clothing, and hairstyle. I was convinced that she liked me, but I was careful not to come on any stronger. I told her that I was looking for my cousin who I thought was living somewhere in the area. I gave her the name and pleaded with her to help me. Though a customer is entitled to confidentiality, privacy laws were a bit more lax at the time of this episode.

I keep spinning my story to the customer service girl. "A good friend of mine told me that he met my cousin at a party and they immediately connected," I said. "She gave him her address but he lost it. He remembered asking her if she still lived on a street with the name of a direction, because since he knew her over the past ten years, she and her husband moved to streets that all had names of a direction. In Ohio, it was Eastern Avenue. In Michigan, it was North Street. In San Francisco, it was West Lane."

Before my mark had a chance to respond, I made sure that she noticed me looking at her gorgeous legs. But instead of saying anything about her legs, I complimented her on her beautiful shoes.

She gave me a coquettish wink, fully aware that I wasn't looking at her shoes.

I continued where I had left off. "I want to pop in and surprise her when she least expects it. Please, you have to help me."

She gave me a sexy smile as she replied. "Let's see if you're right."

I sat in my chair waiting for what seemed like an eternity, trying not to let her see me shaking with nervous anticipation as she checked the database.

At last, the silence was broken. "Mr. Carlos," she said, "I have good news and bad news. Which do you want to hear first?"

"Let's hear the bad news first," I grumbled.

"Are you ready, Mr. Carlos?"

I was ready to toss her in the sack right there but obviously couldn't do such a thing. I'm a married man! "Yes," I said. "Tell me already."

"I'm sorry to disappoint you, sir. She doesn't live on a street with a direction."

At this point, I was busting at the seams. Trying hard to maintain my composure, I blurted out, "What the blazes is the good news?"

"She lives on Merewether Lane."

"Really?" I said. "Wow, you're good."

"I'm very happy that I could help you, sir," she said. I took the liberty of giving her a little peck on the cheek, thanking her at least three times.

I had an address. What could I do with it? I had no proof Mrs. Cobra did the damage. So what possible reason did I have to look for her? I guess it was strictly ego—there was little reason to expect any financial compensation. I'm sure the Cobras had exhausted their resources with all the money they spent on lawyers. But like the saying goes, what goes around comes around. One day she'll pay, hopefully big time

Meanwhile, I received a letter from the Cobras' insurance company demanding me to come to their office to answer questions. Our insurance company representative joined me to hold my hand. At the deposition, two men and one woman sat across from me. I felt like a horse thief sitting before the late Judge Bean, the guy who hung you first and asked questions later. The woman, who had horn-rimmed glasses resting on her nose, was the bad cop. She was very smart, trying hard to make me lose my temper so she could claim I was a violent psychopath, the kind who might destroy his own house to collect the insurance. I made sure not to oblige her, even though she pressed all the right buttons.

Calm as a cucumber, I politely gave her a piece of my mind. "Madam, I don't like you. You're very mean and nasty. Who knows, with your violent temper, maybe *you* tore my house apart?"

"Get the hell out of my office before I call security," She said.

I smiled and looked directly in her eyes. "Have a nice day." I clasped my speechless insurance reps hand and we left the office.

CHAPTER THIRTY-ONE

MRS. CHEETEM

THE HOUSE WAS READY for sale. I erased the word "rental" from my vocabulary. Our broker, Mrs. Cheetem, was an Asian lady with an office a couple miles away from the house. She convinced my wife and I, against our better judgment, to give her an exclusive right to sell. Multiple listing was usually a better choice. But we were in such desperate shape financially that we weren't thinking clearly and succumbed. She had me by the eggs.

Three weeks after our first meeting, we paid her a visit, hoping for some positive results. She told us that we had set the price too high. I reminded her that she had set the price, not us.

She wasn't having any of it. "Yesterday, I ran a computer search for the immediate area, discovering three comparable houses that sold for $50,000 to $75,000 less than yours."

"How come you didn't learn this in the first few days?" I yelped.

"My girl was out sick. I'm sorry about that."

In two weeks, I had to pay some delinquent mortgage money or risk ruining my credit. Now, even if Cheetem found a buyer right then, it was going to take time before we'd go to closing. I was furious.

Adding salt to the wounds, she hit us with a bombshell. "I've grown to love your house. I could make you an offer right now," she said.

My wife and I looked at each other in total shock. Was she playing us all along? Now, are you ready for this? She offered us $100,000 under the listed price. I kicked my wife under the table so she'd stop crying, but to no avail. We didn't know at the time that Mrs. Cheetem had already learned we were way behind in our mortgage payments. After haggling with her for several minutes we finally settled on $90,000 under the listed price. The only good thing was that it was an all cash deal, which allowed us to catch up on some pressing bills. This experience taught me one thing: Even though every broker is required to take a course in ethics, that doesn't mean they have to be there for every class.

We were finally able to breathe. We couldn't wait to close and not have to see her face again.

Two years after selling the house of horror to Mrs. Cheetem, my insurance company made us an offer for the damages that Cobras inflicted. It was at least $70,000 less than it should have been, but seeing as we still were financially stressed, we had to accept it. Now just because I sold the house, you'd think my troubles were over. Think again.

From the first day we bought the house from the Wackos, without our knowledge, random trespassers had cut through the property, crawling through a hole in the backyard fence. The backyard was on the service road of a major expressway. Pedestrians exiting a bus on that expressway saved time by cutting through the backyard. I knew about the rush-hour shortcut, but wasn't aware that if you don't stop such behavior within ten years, trespassers gain the legal right of egress. None of my tenants, including the Cobras, said one word to me about it, so I chose to ignore the subject. But it was a different story with Mrs. Cheetem.

Shortly after the closing, she called me at home, screaming at the top of her lungs. "Why didn't you tell me about the hole in the fence? My little girl was scared to death when she saw an ugly monster in the backyard. You are going to come over here and fix the fence, or you will hear from my lawyer."

She of course had signed a contract specifically stating that the house was being sold "as is." But because we had such an outstanding record in court, I told my wife it behooved us to fix the effing fence and avoid the effing court and avoid having to say things like "Yes, your effing honor," "You're right, your effing honor," and "We will do as you say, your effing honor."

I sent a couple of my guys over there with all the necessary equipment to remove the broken fence and install a new one.

One day later, I got another phone call from the bitch.

"Where did you buy such an ugly fence? At least the other one had some aesthetic value. Go back there and install the right fence."

This was the last straw. I hung up the phone. Without hesitation, I reached into the drawer, pulled out a piece of plain white paper, and wrote the following:

Dear Mrs. Broker,

With regard to the hole in the fence, you can now take the fence, the scary man in the backyard, and anything else back there that I forgot to mention, and shove it all into a place where darkness prevails

Yours truly,

The overly abused, stupid jerks that sold you the house

I saved the receipts for both material and labor on the fence. I also saved the tape recording I made of her second phone call to me, in which she expressed her dissatisfaction. If the reader gets the impression I was slowly becoming insane, he or she is correct. I mailed the letter certified, return receipt requested. I knew that as long as my guys had secured the fence properly, using good material, and closed the opening the trespassers used to cross the yard, she'd get nowhere. I was right for a change.

That was the last time I heard from the bitch. Every now and then, I passed by the house, just to see if there were any changes.

It didn't look like it from the outside, but I can't comment on the inside. You'd think after the low price she paid for the house, she'd at least spend some money to improve the grounds, paint the outside, and replace the rotted wooden shingles clearly visible as you drove by. All this cheap bitch would do was complain about a hole in the fence. I would love to pay her back for the way she set us up.

But as I said at the time to my wife, "Let Lucifer handle it and invite both Mrs. Cobra and Mrs. Cheetem to a barbeque."

Seventeen years later, I was reading the newspaper in the breakfast room of my home when I saw on one of the back pages an article of interest. It was about a couple that had been arrested for bilking an insurance company. I read on. They somehow fooled the insurance company, claiming to be the owners of the house when in fact they were only tenants. A witness claimed that he had seen, from his kitchen window, the couple ripping off wallpaper from the walls and a man hammering several times what appeared to be a dishwasher. I read on. Once the insurance company found out, they immediately pressed charges. The couple was indicted but the article didn't mention their names.

The article was continued on the next page. I flipped the page and saw an unclear photograph of the couple accused of fraud. I couldn't recognize the faces, even with a magnifying glass. I didn't feel like pursuing the matter, so I put it behind me. If I had found out it was the Cobras, it would only have rekindled a flame that I wanted to keep unlit forever.

CHAPTER THIRTY-TWO

THE DEVIL

THE FOLLOWING MORNING, I met Lucifer for the first time. He was sitting on a park bench minding his own business and barbecuing someone's intestines. I guess he must have felt lonely, because he invited me to sit down and share his hand-cooked delicacy.

It was hard for me to resist, but I took a rain check on the intestines. Lucifer was a pleasant chap, not at all like I thought he would be. We shot the breeze for a few minutes and then he asked me in a gentle tone of voice whether I would be interested in returning with him to his domain.

I expressed my concern that I wouldn't find the surroundings suitable.

He completely understood. He asked me if I knew of someone else that might accept his invitation.

Without hesitating, I answered yes.

"Can you tell me their names?"

I'll try to accommodate you, sir, but there are so many people who used me for a punching bag, toilet bowl, tainted urinal, soccer ball and javelin, it would be almost impossible to list them all. But there are two people in particular . . ."

"Who might they be? Lucifer asked, his tongue hanging out in eager anticipation.

"Cobra and Cheetem," I answered.

Lucifer flinched. "Oh, I know these ladies. They were in my domain for many years, but they needed more experience in how to interact with people, so I sent them up here a few years ago for training."

"I think they have passed the test, Mr. Lucifer. You can recall them," I said.

"Thank you, Mr. Carlos," he said. "I'll look into it."

We shook hands and went our separate ways. The third-degree burn I suffered from the handshake was worth it knowing that I could sit down with the ruler of hell and have him treat me with such courtesy. There's no reason to think we can't be friends. I still have his business card, which lists the direct line to his office: 1-800-GO2-HELL.

THE END